D1109901

A BASIC GUIDE TO
Wrestling

An Official U.S. Olympic Committee Sports Series

The U.S. Olympic Committee

Griffin Publishing Group

This Hardcover Edition Distributed By
Gareth Stevens Publishing
A World Almanac Education Group Company

Published by Griffin Publishing Group under license from the United States Olympic Committee.

The use of the Olympic-related marks and terminology is authorized by the United States Olympic Committee pursuant to 36 USC 220506.

This hardcover edition distributed by
Gareth Stevens Publishing
A World Almanac Education Group Company
330 West Olive Street, Suite 100
Milwaukee, WI 53212 USA

For a free color catalog describing Gareth Stevens' list of high-quality books and multimedia programs, call 1-800-542-2595 (USA) or 1-800-461-9120 (Canada). Gareth Stevens Publishing's Fax: (414) 332-3567.
Visit Gareth Stevens' website at: www.garethstevens.com

Library of Congress Cataloging-in-Publication Data for this hardcover edition available upon request from Gareth Stevens Publishing. Fax: (414) 336-0157 for the attention of the Publishing Records Department.

Hardcover edition: ISBN 0-8368-2799-6

Editorial Statement
In the interest of brevity, the Editors have chosen to use the standard English form of address. Please be advised that this usage is not meant to suggest a restriction to, nor an endorsement of, any individual or group of individuals, either by age, gender, or athletic ability. The Editors certainly acknowledge that boys and girls, men and women, of every age and physical condition are actively involved in sports, and we encourage everyone to enjoy the sports of his or her choice.

1 2 3 4 5 6 7 8 9 05 04 03 02 01

Printed in the United States of America

ACKNOWLEDGMENTS

PUBLISHER — Griffin Publishing Group
DIR. / OPERATIONS — Robin L. Howland
PROJECT MANAGER — Bryan K. Howland
WRITER — Suzanne Ledeboer
BOOK DESIGN — Midnight Media

USOC
CHAIRMAN/PRESIDENT — William J. Hybl

USA WRESTLING
PRESIDENT — Jeff Blatnik
EXECUTIVE DIRECTOR — Jim Scherr

EDITORS — Geoffrey M. Horn
Catherine Gardner
PHOTOS — USA Wrestling /Heather Van Peursem
Bob Dunlop
Staatliche Museum of Berlin
National Park Service
Casey B. Gibson
Dick McCoy/Thumbs Up
Lloyd Ostendof
National Federation of State High School Associations
National Collegiate Athletic Association
COVER DESIGN — m2design group
COVER PHOTO — ©Digital Vision, Ltd.

Special thanks to USA Wrestling for the use of
biography information and athlete photos.

The United States Olympic Committee

The U.S. Olympic Committee (USOC) is the custodian of the U.S. Olympic Movement and is dedicated to providing opportunities for American athletes of all ages.

The USOC, a streamlined organization of member organizations, is the moving force for support of sports in the United States that are on the program of the Olympic and/or Pan American Games, or those wishing to be included.

The USOC has been recognized by the International Olympic Committee since 1894 as the sole agency in the United States whose mission involves training, entering, and underwriting the full expenses for the United States teams in the Olympic and Pan American Games. The USOC also supports the bid of U.S. cities to host the winter and summer Olympic Games, or the winter and summer Pan American Games, and after reviewing all the candidates, votes on and may endorse one city per event as the U.S. bid city. The USOC also approves the U.S. trial sites for the Olympic and Pan American Games team selections.

WELCOME TO THE OLYMPIC SPORTS SERIES

We feel this unique series will encourage parents, athletes of all ages, and novices who are thinking about a sport for the first time to get involved with the challenging and rewarding world of Olympic sports.

This series of Olympic sport books covers both summer and winter sports, features Olympic history and basic sports fundamentals, and encourages family involvement. Each book includes information on how to get started in a particular sport, including equipment and clothing; rules of the game; health and fitness; basic first aid; and guidelines for spectators. Of special interest is the information on opportunities for senior citizens, volunteers, and physically challenged athletes. In addition, each book is enhanced by photographs and illustrations and a complete, easy-to-understand glossary.

Because this family-oriented series neither assumes nor requires prior knowledge of a particular sport, it can be enjoyed by all age groups. Regardless of anyone's level of sports knowledge, playing experience, or athletic ability, this official U.S. Olympic Committee Sports Series will encourage understanding and participation in sports and fitness.

The purchase of these books will assist the U.S. Olympic Team. This series supports the Olympic mission and serves importantly to enhance participation in the Olympic and Pan American Games.

United States Olympic Committee

Contents

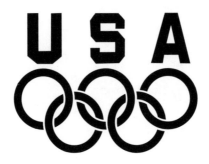

AN ATHLETE'S CREED

The most important thing in the Olympic Games is not to win but to take part, just as the most important thing in life is not the triumph but the struggle. The essential thing is not to have conquered but to have fought well.

These famous words, commonly referred to as the Olympic Creed, were once spoken by Baron Pierre de Coubertin, founder of the modern Olympic Games. Whatever their origins, they aptly describe the theme behind each and every Olympic competition.

Metric Equivalents

Wherever possible, measurements given are those specified by the Olympic rules. Other measurements are given in metric or standard U.S. units, as appropriate. For purposes of comparison, the following rough equivalents may be used.

1 kilometer (km)	= 0.62 mile (mi)	1 mi = 1.61 km
1 meter (m)	= 3.28 feet (ft)	1 ft = 0.305 m
	= 1.09 yards (yd)	1 yd = 0.91 m
1 centimeter (cm)	= 0.39 inch (in)	1 in = 2.54 cm
	= 0.1 hand	1 hand (4 in) = 10.2 cm
1 kilogram (kg)	= 2.2 pounds (lb)	1 lb = 0.45 kg
1 milliliter (ml)	= 0.03 fluid ounce (fl oz)	1 fl oz = 29.573 ml
1 liter	= 0.26 gallons (gal)	1 gal = 3.785 liters

1

Wrestling and the Olympics

Originally a survival skill, wrestling is probably the world's oldest competitive sport, with both an ancient and a modern history, and it continues to be a way to develop the physical skills of young people. Wrestling entered the Ancient Olympic Games at the 18th Olympiad in 708 B.C., where it remained an event for nearly five centuries. Although wrestling's modern history in the Games dates from 1896, its origins date to prehistory and early recorded time.

Wrestling's Heritage

There is no exact date for the origin of wrestling, but many ancient civilizations have left evidence of the sport in tomb carvings and written documents. Caves in France have carvings and drawings, dating back 15,000-20,000 years, showing wrestlers in the common positions known to the modern world. The Sumerians left similar evidence on stone slabs nearly 5,000 years ago. Mythic stories tell of Gilgamesh, a ruler and protector of ancient Sumeria, who fought a bull to save the city of Uruk and used his great strength to subdue opponents—often his enemies—who then became his friends and supporters. Pictorial evidence unearthed from the ancient civilizations of China, Japan, Babylonia, and Greece reveal glimpses of traditional wrestling, as do some Egyptian hieroglyphics dating back to about 2400 B.C. The tomb of Vizier Ptahhotep shows six different wrestling holds, for example. At the temple-tomb of Beni Hasan near the Nile River in Egypt, tomb carvings depict over 200 wrestlers, many in positions that are still practiced and used by wrestlers today. Students of gymnastics practiced wrestling as one in a series of body-building exercises, yet wrestling retained its separate identity as a sport.

Even Greek gods wrestled. The poet Pindar described how the gods Zeus and Kronus wrestled for possession of the universe, and the first Olympic festival in 776 B.C. was held to commemorate Zeus' victory. In the *Iliad,* Homer described a wrestling match between Odysseus and Ajax. Plato, meaning "broad shoulders," was the nickname given to the philosopher because as a young man he had won so many wrestling matches. (His real name was Aristocles.) In Greece, young men attended wrestling schools, which were social centers and the place to learn battle skills.

Wrestling in the Ancient Olympic Games

Wrestling entered the Ancient Olympic Games in 708 B.C. and proved to be a huge popular success. Although discus throwers were the most popular Olympic athletes, wrestlers were second and had their own fans. Milo of Croton, the famous wrestler of antiquity, had 32 victories, which included winning six Olympic championships in a row. When he wasn't competing, Milo was well-known for his lifestyle. He carried an ox around his shoulders, broke cords tied around his neck by tensing his neck muscles, and consumed prodigious amounts of food and drink.

Ancient Wrestling Styles

Theseus, the legendary Athenian hero and slayer of the Minotaur, is credited in Greek tradition with the invention of wrestling and the rules governing the sport. Regardless of the inventor, there is no question that wrestling was important to those ancient Greek athletes, who participated in two forms of the sport—upright and pancratium.

Upright

Upright wrestling was the final, deciding event of ancient pentathlon and was similar to modern freestyle wrestling, with no holds allowed above the waist.

Pancratium

Pancratium was a "no-holds-barred" form with boxing, hitting, and kicking allowed. It was permissible to twist your opponent's arms and legs and strangle him, but biting and gouging (presumably of eyes) were forbidden. The match had no time limit, but ended whenever one of the wrestlers gave up and admitted defeat.

In Asia and the Americas

When the Mongols conquered India in A.D. 1526, they brought a style of wrestling known as "loose," which has evolved into the form used in Pakistan and India today. Loose wrestling begins with the opponents separated, and they are allowed to start with any permitted legal hold they choose. The style is similar to Japan's especially in the size of the competitors and the range and finesse of their moves.

The Chinese, by 700 B.C., also competed in loose wrestling, which they probably learned from those same Mongols who later conquered India. The Japanese recorded their first wrestling bout in 23 B.C. The winner, Sukune, is the ancient model for all Japanese wrestlers. Sumo, as the sport is known, became part of annual harvest festivals in Japan; it is said that two brothers wrestled for the imperial throne. We also know that centuries before Europeans explored and inhabited the Western Hemisphere, Native Americans wrestled with enemy tribes and wrestled for sport at their festivals.

Wrestling in the Middle Ages

After the Roman conquest of the Greeks, wrestling declined from a sport into a brutal contest for some competitors. Nevertheless, the sport continued to spread with the Roman Empire across Europe. About A.D. 800, wrestling enjoyed a resurgence as a sporting competition when knights of the Holy Roman Empire became skilled in its forms and engaged men from other countries in bouts. In the years before printed information was widely available, medieval knights followed handwritten wrestling instructions, including sketches, to guide their training.

The British were fierce regional rivals, and their first recorded wrestling match occurred in London between wrestlers from Cornwall and Devon in the thirteenth century. Two rival monarchs were well known for their wrestling ability and patronage of the sport. It is reported that Francis I, King of France, once challenged King Henry VII of England to a friendly bout, which Henry lost, to his great discomfort.

Regional Styles

Other countries developed wrestling as a competitive sport with their own unique regional styles. The Persian Empire—Iran, today—learned wrestling from Turkish soldiers about A.D. 800, using a style known as *koresh*. Opponents wore leather pants that were long and tight and could be gripped by their opponent. *Koresh* is a variation of the loose style and spread as the Turks dominated the area. Today, it is the national sport of Iran, as sumo is in Japan.

Sumo *is* unique. Opponents, whose weights may top 300 pounds, try to *throw* one another to the ground or force one another out of a 4.6-meter circular pit filled with sand. (It isn't necessary to pin your opponent in order to win.) The contests usually don't last very long, as the wrestlers, in spite of their huge size, are very quick on their feet. A sumo bout ends when one of the competitors touches the ground with any part of his body, except his feet.

In modern Japan, sumo has millions of loyal fans—from the very young to retirees—who watch the national tournaments, called *bashos,* on prime-time TV and in person. The sport is more popular than baseball, makes the front pages of newspapers, and draws audiences the way a World Series or Super Bowl does in the United States.

British regional wrestling styles drew their names from the districts where the style began, in Devon, Cornwall, Cumberland, Westmoreland, and Lancashire, the last of which played a part in the development of freestyle wrestling. In Devon, the old rules allowed you to wear sturdy shoes and kick your opponent's shins, while in Cumberland, if you lost your starting hold, or if any part of your body touched the ground, except your feet, you lost. Wrestlers in Cornwall wore a canvas jacket but were not allowed to strangle their opponents with the jacket collar! That was strictly forbidden.

Development of Modern Wrestling

For centuries, wrestling remained local and regional, an individual sport with little or no organization for serious competitors. Not until the end of the nineteenth century, and the early years of the twentieth, would wrestling achieve the recognition and acquire the organization needed to make it an international sport.

During the eighteenth and nineteenth centuries, wrestling matches were common events at circuses, fairs, and expositions, attracting large crowds of fans and those who were simply curious. As a young man growing up and working in New Salem, IL, Abraham Lincoln was a well-known local wrestler famous for "thrashing" his opponents. Presidents George Washington and William Howard Taft were wrestlers of some note, with Washington reportedly taking on seven challengers in a row and defeating them all. Wrestlers came in all sizes, shapes, and weights, and their bouts were played in a variety of styles, but the most popular were Greco-Roman and freestyle.

Modern Styles and Variations

Greco-Roman

Early in the nineteenth century, the French developed the modern wrestling style known as Greco-Roman based on modifications to the style used by the ancient Greeks. Unlike freestyle, in Greco-Roman competition a wrestler cannot use his legs to attack his opponent, and no holds are allowed below the waist. You may not trip or squeeze with your legs, or push, press, or lift. Legs are for support and lifting. Therefore, upper-body strength and leverage are required to perfect this wrestling style. Greco-Roman was the only form of wrestling event in the modern Olympic Games until 1904, when freestyle was added. Since 1920, both have been contested at the Olympic Games and other national and international competitions.

Freestyle

Freestyle is the descendant of ancient Greek upright wrestling and the Lancashire regional style, in which no holds were barred. Then, tripping was allowed, and throwing your opponent to the ground three times made you the victor.

Courtesy Lloyd Ostendof

Abraham Lincoln wrestling Jack Armstrong to a draw

You could use your legs to make single-leg or double-leg tackles, but a scissors lock on the neck, head, or body of your opponent was forbidden. (One major difference today is that wrestlers no longer rub themselves with oil and fine sand to get better holds!) Freestyle wrestling, with some modifications, is the style used in most parts of the world and remains the most popular form in North America (see Chapter 4, "The Match").

Folkstyles

Besides Greco-Roman and freestyle, there are some 160 folkstyle, or folklore, wrestling forms practiced throughout the world. The Swiss use a style of wrestling known as

National Park Service

A young William Howard Taft

schwingen (swinging) and wear special pants with strong belts. Wrestlers begin by gripping one another's belts and can lift and trip. Iceland's *glima* style makes use of belts and is popular in Syria, while the former Soviet Republics follow many different regional folkstyles, all forms of "belt and jacket" wrestling. The United States has its own folkstyle wrestling, which is practiced in high school and colleges.

Organizing the Sport

Prior to 1924, styles, divisions, and rules varied at each Olympic Games. It seemed that the host nations favored the styles perfected by their own athletes; therefore, the best wrestlers were often hard to identify. Some common organization seemed desirable, so individuals concerned with the future of the sport founded the *Fédération Internationale des Luttes Associées* (FILA) in 1912. FILA became the international governing body for amateur wrestling, giving the sport rules, standards, and organized competitions. This seemed to be the turning point, because thereafter amateur wrestling and wrestling bouts increased in popularity throughout the world.

The Modern Olympic Games

Scandinavians dominated the sport in the first half of the twentieth century; from 1908 until 1948, wrestlers from Sweden and Finland usually won the medals in the Greco-Roman events at the Olympic Games. The only off-year for the Finns was 1928, when a German won in Greco-Roman; however, Finns were the overall winners. These early twentieth-century wrestling events often had no time periods, so it was not unusual for matches to last for hours. One six-hour marathon bout at Stockholm in 1912 ended with no decision for the two Finnish Greco-Roman wrestlers, an exhausting event that day for everyone. The United States dominated in freestyle wrestling competitions at the beginning of the century and has won the most medals of any nation in this style during the last 100 years.

At the London Games (1948), 27 nations, with a total of 266 athletes competed. Henry Wittenberg, a New York policeman with a string of 300 undefeated bouts, won a gold, although most medals went to wrestlers from Turkey and Sweden.

Turkey lost an opportunity to repeat its 1948 win at Helsinki (1952) when its entry forms, for some unknown reason, were delayed. This mishap gave first-time Soviet competitors their opportunity. They used it well, performing best in Greco-Roman and in the total number of medals won by their wrestlers. The 1956 Games in Melbourne saw the Soviets return and build on their 1952 victories by repeating in Greco-Roman and in the overall total of medals won in wrestling.

Rome (1960) was the perfect city for this ancient sport, dominated that year by West Germany's Wilfried Dietrich. But it was also a year for the United States wrestlers to shine; in addition, competitors from Eastern Bloc nations began to dominate. The Soviet Union's Alexander Medved won three gold medals in a row—at Tokyo (1964), at Mexico City (1968), and at Munich (1972)—a first in the history of modern wrestling at the Olympic Games.

During 1972-1980, Eastern Bloc nations and the Soviet Union continued to excel in all classes of wrestling, even having repeat winners, but never a three-in-a-row like Medved until 1996, when Russia's Alexander Karelin won his third straight in Greco-Roman. A victory pleasing to most fans in 1980 was that of Sylianos Mygiakis of Greece—the first Greek in modern times to win a gold in Greco-Roman.

Beginning in the 1980s under Milan Ercegan of Yugoslavia, the president of FILA, "total wrestling" for international competitions was instituted. The bouts are shorter—down from nine minutes to five minutes, or two three-minute periods—and they are aggressive, not passive. (Penalties may be assessed if you are a passive participant.) Universal wrestling is included in total wrestling; it requires new techniques with varied actions and holds. The modern thrust is risk; from the 1980's onward, Olympic Games wrestling was to be active, fast, and athletic.

At Los Angeles in 1984, the United States probably had its best-ever freestyle wrestling team, coached by Dan Gable, the 1972 Olympic Games gold medalist. Brothers Ed and Lou Banach and Dave and Mark Schultz each won a gold. An extra-special moment for wrestler Jeff Blatnick, who had overcome Hodgkin's disease, was his gold medal in Greco-Roman. The Soviet Bloc boycotted the 1984 Games, as the United States had done in 1980, so the opportunity for head-to-head competition between those two strong teams was lost.

The 1988 Games (Seoul) saw the USSR on top in all classes—freestyle, Greco-Roman, and overall medal winner. Four years later in Barcelona, competing as the Unified Team, the former Eastern Bloc countries repeated as wrestling champions in all classes. The United States had a strong team, but there were challenges from newcomers: South Korea, North Korea, and Cuba in freestyle; Norway, Turkey, Hungary, Germany, Cuba, and South Korea in the Greco-Roman events.

At the Centennial Olympic Games in Atlanta, the United States won more medals in freestyle wrestling than any other country and had the highest overall medal total for its wrestlers.

Every year since 1930, the James E. Sullivan Memorial Trophy (named after the former president of the Amateur Athletic Union) is awarded to an American athlete whose performance, example, and influence as an amateur have done the most during the year to advance the cause of sportsmanship in the United States. In 1990, two-time Olympic champion wrestler John Smith received the Sullivan award; in March 1996, the award went to Bruce Baumgartner, gold-medal winner of the 130 kg in freestyle at the Los Angeles and Barcelona Olympic Games.

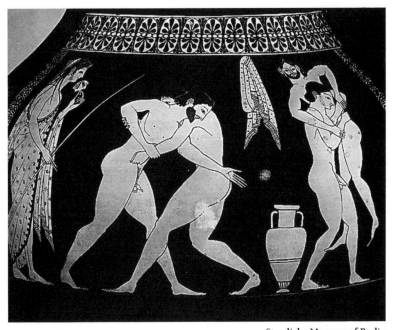

Staatliche Museum of Berlin

Wrestlers on a fifth century vase

Weight/Age Classes
International Competitions
Greco-Roman and Freestyle Events
FILA and USA Wrestling

Senior Men (20 years and older)   48-130 kg
(Wrestlers in the Junior age group can wrestle with the senior age group)
Senior Women (20 years and older)   41-75 kg
(16-19 year-olds need medical certificate)
Juniors (ages 18-20)   46-130 kg
(17 years with medical certificate)

International Competitions
Greco-Roman and Freestyle

Senior Men
• International events
• Continental championships and cups each year
• World Championships and cups year apart from Olympic Games years
• Challenge bouts, Masters, International Grand Prix, FILA Gala Grand Prix, Super Stars bouts
• Olympic Games

Wrestlers in the Junior category may participate in a Senior competition. However, they must be at least 17 years of age in the year in which the event is held. Also, they must be sponsored by their National Federation and present an authorized medical certificate in order to participate.

Junior Men
• International competitions

- Continental championships each year
- World Championships each year

Wrestlers who are at least 17 years of age in the year in which the event is held may participate in Junior Men competitions. However, they must be "under the responsibility of their Federation" and must present an authorized medical certificate in order to participate.

Schoolboys

- Bilateral and regional international competitions

(USAW age groups and competitions differ)

Women's Wrestling

The Spartans of ancient Greece trained young women in the art of wrestling, but they were not part of the ancient Olympic Games and did not have a legendary role model until the third century A.D. Zenobia, Queen of Palmyra, was a strong ruler who occupied Egypt and was well known for her skill at the sport. Wrestling for women has a sketchy history, at best, and did not appear as a recognized sport until recently.

When women take up the sport, getting started often means that a female is the lone member of a traditional all-male team and competes against young men. This can be difficult and requires above-average determination and dedication. In spite of the obstacles, more and more preteen girls as young as seven or eight, as well as women in their early twenties, are wrestling and competing at local, regional, state, national, and international competitions. The U.S. Nationals, for example, grew from 20 entrants in its initial year to 120 for the 1995 tournament.

Women wrestlers at competitions follow the same rules as men, can earn the same points, and are prohibited from making the same illegal holds, all double nelsons, in *par terre* or a standing position, there is no clinch in women's wrestling. The age categories and weight classes, as established by FILA and USA Wrestling, are different for women's wrestling, as are the dress code and some rules. For complete charts and details, consult the most recent edition of the *International Rule Book and Guide to Wrestling*.

More and more international competitions are open to women. Since 1989, American women wrestlers have competed in the Women's World Championships. Japanese

Casey B. Gibson

Sheri Belew-Kennedy at the 1996 U.S. Nationals

women lead the world at these games, followed by female wrestlers from Norway, France, Russia, the United States, and China. However, the Americans are catching up: Tricia Saunders of Phoenix, AZ, has won two World titles, and Shannon Williams of Ontario, CA, has earned four world medals.

To boost the development of women wrestlers, USA Wrestling (USAW), the official governing body for amateur

Casey B. Gibson

Tricia Saunders at the 1996 U.S. Nationals

wrestling in the United States, sponsored its first Junior Women's Tour du Monde in the summer of 1995. This tour is for young wrestlers who are at the top of their age group, and six traveled to Sweden to train with other young women wrestlers and compete in a mini-tournament. This was not a vacation from training! Each day, the participants swam, ran track, did gymnastics drills, ran cross-country, did hill running, and worked out on the mat. However, they did have time to enjoy a number of cultural events with their Scandinavian hosts.

That year USAW held its first development camp for women. The enthusiastic participants worked with top coaches and athletes to improve their wrestling skills. In 1996, USA Wrestling hosted its first Cadet Women's Nationals for athletes 14 to 16 years old.

In addition, USAW has developed a Women's Team USA program, which is the national team for women wrestlers. Top competitors included Vickie Zummo (97 lb), Shannon Williams (116.5 lb), and Tricia Saunders (103.5 lb), who has won seven national championships already. When Saunders isn't winning championships, she works as a bacteriologist.

In less than a decade, young women wrestlers have begun to build their reputations in the sport and are proving that they can enter, compete, and win at national and international events. With increased support from families, coaches, FILA, and USAW, their medal total is bound to go up. Many observers expect that women's wrestling will soon gain the status of a medal sport at the Olympic Games.

1999-2000 Women's Team USA

46 kg/101.25 lb
1. Tricia Saunders, Phoenix, AZ (Sunkist Kids)
2. Olivia Ocampo, Oxnard, CA (UM-Morris)
3. Julie Gonzales, Vallejo, CA (Peninsula Grapplers)

51 kg/112.25 lb
1. Stephanie Murata, Boca Raton, FL (Sunkist Kids)
2. Malissa Sherwood, Rocklin, CA (Dave Schultz WC)
3. Patricia Miranda, Saratoga, CA (Dave Schultz WC)

56 kg/123.25 lb
1. Tina George, Colorado Springs, CO
   (Minnesota Storm)
2. Sara McMann, Marion, NC (UM-Morris)
3. Afsoon Johnston, Phoenix, AZ (Sunkist Kids)

62 kg/136.5 lb
1. Lauren Wolfe, Troy, NY (Michigan WC)
2. Jimi Dawn Hornbuckle, Lawrence, KS
   (Dave Schultz WC)
3. Megan Andrews, Napa, CA (Peninsula Grapplers)

68 kg/149.75 lb
1. Sandra Bacher, San Jose, CA (Dave Schultz WC)
2. Katie Downing, Pendleton, IN (UM-Morris)
3. Tonya Evinger, Bates City, MO (Wrestling Central)

75 kg/165.25 lb
1. Kristie Stenglein, Albany, NY (ATWA)
2. Iris Smith, Colorado Springs, CP
3. Dominique Smalley, Iowa City, IA (Dave Schultz WC)

Meet the U.S. Wrestlers

USA Wrestling

President
Jeff Blatnik

Freestyle Biographies

Sammie Henson	54kg/119 lb
Terry Brands	58kg/127.75 lb
Cary Kolat	63kg/138.75 lb
Lincoln McIlravy	69kg/152 lb
Brandon Slay	76kg/167.5 lb
Charles Burton	85kg/187.25 lb
Melvin Douglas	97kg/213.75 lb
Kerry McCoy	130kg/286 lb

Greco-Roman Biographies

Steven Mays	54kg/119 lb
Jim Gruenwald	58kg/127.75 lb

Kevin Bracken	63kg/138.75 lb
Heath Sims	69kg/152 lb
Matt Lindland	76kg/167.5 lb
Quincey Clark	85kg/187.25 lb
Garrett Lowney	97kg/213.75 lb
Rulon Gardner	130kg/286 lb

Jeff Blatnick

In 1984, Jeff Blatnick emerged as one of the most inspirational Olympic heroes in history. Two years after being diagnosed with Hodgkin's disease and undergoing surgery and radiation therapy, he continued his pursuit of an Olympic medal in the super heavyweight division of Greco-Roman wrestling. An overwhelming underdog when the tournament began, he upset Thomas Johaneson in the final to win the gold medal, the first U.S. medal of any kind in Greco-Roman wrestling. During his sixteen-year wrestling career, Blatnick won ten national titles and various international awards. Blatnick was a member of both the 1980 and 1984 U.S. Olympic teams, and retired from competition in 1988.

Since then, in addition to his motivational speaking engagements, Blatnick has worked as a television commentator for various networks. He has appeared as an expert analyst on NBC, ABC, ESPN, MSG Network, and Prime Ticket Cable.

He is currently the president of USA Wrestling and is involved with the President's program for Physical Fitness and Sport. For his volunteer efforts, Blatnick, a 1979 graduate of Springfield College, has received numerous honors for his volunteer efforts, including U.S.A. Wrestling's 1985 Man of the Year.

USA Wrestling

Freestyle

SAMMIE HENSON

2000-01 Team USA Ranking:
Ranked 1st at 54 kg/119 lb

Years on Team USA: 5
(1994-96, 97-00)

Residence: Norman, OK

Club: Sunkist Kids

College: Clemson Univ., Univ.
of Missouri

High School: St. Charles, MO
(Francis Howell HS)

Born: January 1, 1971, in St.
Louis, MO

Height: 5' 4"

International Competition: Second in 2000 Cerro Pelado
Tournament (Cuba)... 2000 Olympic Qualifying Tournament
champion (Belarus)... Second in 1999 Clansman International
(Canada)... Fourth in 1999 Sunkist Kids/ASU International
Open... Second in 1998-99 World Cup... 1999 Yasar Dogu
champion (Turkey)... 1998 World Champion... Second in
1998 Goodwill Games... Sixth in 1998 Yasar Dogu
Tournament (Turkey)... Third in 1998 Kiev Grand Prix
(Ukraine)... Second in 1997 Uzbekistan Cup... 1997 Yasar
Dogu Tournament champion (Turkey)... Third in 1996 Henri
Deglane Challenge (France)... Third in 1996 Kiev Grand Prix

(Ukraine)... Fourth in 1996 Yarygin Tournament (Russia)... Third in 1994 and 1996 Sunkist International Open... Second in 1993 Pan American Championships... Third in 1990 Pan American Championships in Greco-Roman... Fourth in 1990 Concord Cup in Greco-Roman... 1988 Junior World Team member in Greco-Roman...

U.S. Competition: 1998 and 2000 U.S. Nationals champion... NYAC Christmas Open Champion... Fourth in 1999 World Team Trials... 1998 World Team Trials champion...... Second in 1997 World Team Trials... Second in 1997 U.S. Nationals... Third in 1994-95 World Team Trials... Fourth in 1995 U.S. Nationals... Sixth in 1995 University Nationals... Fifth in 1994 U.S. Nationals... 1993 University Nationals champion... Second in 1992 Olympic Team Trials in Greco-Roman... Third in 1992 U.S. Nationals in Greco-Roman... Second in 1990 World Team Trials in Greco-Roman... 1990 U.S. Nationals champion in Greco-Roman... 1990 U.S. Olympic Festival champion in Greco-Roman... 1990 Espoir Nationals champion in Greco-Roman... Second in 1989 Junior Nationals in Greco-Roman... 1987-88 Junior Nationals champion in Greco-Roman... Fourth in 1988 Final Olympic Qualifier in Greco-Roman... Fourth in 1988 U.S. Nationals in Greco-Roman... Fifth in 1987 Junior Nationals...

College: Competed for Gil Sanchez at Clemson University... 1993 and 1994 NCAA champion as a junior and senior... Also attended the Univ. of Missouri, where he competed for Wes Roper... He placed fifth in 1991 NCAA meet as a freshman... He studied park, recreation, and tourism at Missouri... He is taking graduate classes in human resources...

High School: Competed for Roger Hodapp and Jud Hoffman at Francis Howell High School in Missouri... Won state titles in 1987-89, as a sophomore, junior, and senior... Placed fourth in 1986 state meet as a freshman...

Personal: Works as an assistant wrestling coach at the Univ. Oklahoma... Previously worked as an assistant coach at Univ. of Missouri and Univ. of Northern Iowa... Member of Greco-Roman Team USA in 1990-91 and 1992-93... His wife is Stephanie, they have a newborn son, Jackson.... Hobbies include hiking, basketball and water sports... Henson qualified for the 1988 Final Olympic Trials in Greco-Roman wrestling, while still just a junior in high school...

Awards: 1998 USA Wrestling Freestyle Wrestler of the Year... 1998 USOC Freestyle Wrestler of the Year... 1998 Freestyle Championship Belt Series winner... USOC Athlete of the Month for September 1998... Outstanding Wrestler at 1988 Junior National Championships in Greco-Roman.

TERRY BRANDS

2000-01 Team USA Ranking: No. 1 at 58 kg/127.75 lb

Years on Team USA: 7 (1993-98, 99-01)

Residence: Iowa City, IA

Club: Hawkeye WC

College: Univ. of Iowa

High School: Sheldon, IA (Community HS)

Born: April 9, 1968 in Omaha, NE

Height: 5' 4"

International Competition: Eighth in 1999 Kiev Grand Prix (Ukraine)... 1999 Manitoba Open champion... 1998 Clansman International Open champion... 1993 and 1995

World Champion... 1994-95 World Cup champion... 1995 Pan American Games champion... Seventh in 1995 Cerro Pelado Tournament (Cuba)... Second in 1995 Yarygin Tournament (Russia)... Member of 1994 U.S. World Team... Second in 1993 Krasnoyarsk Tournament (Russia)... Third in 1991 U.S. Open International...

U.S. Competition: 2000 U.S. Olympic Team Trials Champion... 1993-95, 1997 and 1999 World Team Trials champion... 1994 , 1997 and 1999 U.S. Nationals champion... Second in 1996 U.S. Olympic Team Trials... Second in 1993, 1995-96 U.S. Nationals... Fourth in 1992 Olympic Team Trials... Third in the 1992 U.S. Nationals... 1991 U.S. Olympic Festival champion... 1988 Espoir Nationals runner-up... Third in 1987 Junior Nationals... Fifth in 1986 Junior Nationals...

College: Competed for Dan Gable at Univ. of Iowa... 1992 NCAA champion as a senior... 1991 NCAA runner-up as a junior... 1990 NCAA champion as a sophomore... Graduated in 1993 with degree in general studies with emphasis on sport and human development...

High School: Competed for Galen Nelson at Sheldon Community HS in Iowa... 1987 state runner-up as a senior... 1985 and 1986 state champion as a sophomore and junior... Also played football and baseball...

Personal: Twin brother, Tom, won the 136.5 lb. gold medal at the 1996 Olympic Games in Atlanta, GA... Terry and Tom won World titles in 1993, making the Brands twins the first U.S. brothers to win World gold medals the same year... Works as an assistant coach at the Univ. of Nebraska... Former assistant coach at the Univ. of Iowa... Hobbies include rifle, pistol and shotgun shooting, hunting, and outdoor activities... Has a Norwegian Elkhound and Schipperke dog... Wife's name is Michelle ... Has a son, Nelson Ray, and a newborn daughter, Sydney Jae...

Awards: 1995 Championship Belt Series winner... He and brother Tom were named the 1993 USA Wrestling Athletes of the Year, and also the John Smith Award winners as Freestyle Wrestlers of the Year... Along with brother Tom, he received the 1993 Amateur Wrestling News Man of the Year award...

Note: Brands qualified for the 1997 and 1999 U.S. World teams, but was unable to compete in the World Championships due to injury... Did not compete in the 1997-98 season due to injury.

CARY KOLAT

2000-01 Team USA Ranking: Ranked 1st at 63 kg/138.75 lb

Years on Team USA: 6 (1993-94, 95-96, 97-00)

Residence: Morgantown, WV

Club: Dave Schultz WC

College: Lock Haven Univ.

High School: Rices Landing, PA (Jefferson-Morgan HS)

Born: May 19, 1973, in Rices Landing, PA

Height: 5' 5"

International Competition: 2000 Pan American Championships champion... Second in 2000 Poland Open... 1998-99 and 2000 World Cup champion... Fourth in 1999 World Championships... 1999 Pan American Games champion... 1999 Cerro Pelado Tournament champion

(Cuba)... Third in 1998 World Championships... 1998 Goodwill Games champion... 1998 Yasar Dogu Tournament champion (Turkey)... Seventh in 1998 Kiev Grand Prix (Ukraine)... 1991, 1994 and 1997 Henri Deglane Challenge champion (France) ... Second in 1997 World Championships... 1995 Sunkist International Open champion... Second in 1993 Sunkist International Open... 1993 U.S. Open Grand Prix champion... Third in 1992 Canada Cup... Fifth in 1991 U.S. Open International... 1989 Cadet World Champion...

U.S. Competition: 1997, 1999 and 2000 U.S. Nationals champion... 1997-99 World Team Trials champion... Fourth in 1996 U.S. Olympic Team Trials... 1995 U.S. Olympic Festival champion... Third in 1993 and 1995 World Team Trials... Sixth in 1995 U.S. Nationals... 1995 University Nationals champion... 1994 NYAC Open champion... Fifth in 1992 Olympic Team Trials... Fifth in 1992 U.S. Nationals... Fourth in 1991 U.S. Nationals... 1989 Cadet Nationals champion in both styles... 1988 Cadet Nationals freestyle champion...

College: Competed for Carl Poff at Lock Haven Univ. where he was a 1996-97 NCAA champion... He studied sociology and criminology... Competed for John Fritz at Penn State Univ., where he was third in 1994 NCAA Championships as a sophomore and second in 1993 NCAA meet as a freshman...

High School: Competed for Ron Headlee at Jefferson-Morgan High School in Pennsylvania... Four-time state champion (1989-92), with a 137-0 career high school record... Third in 1989 and 1990 Midlands Tournament as a high school wrestler...

Personal: Works as an assistant wrestling coach at the University of West Virginia... Previously he was an assistant coach at the Univ. of Wisconsin, Lehigh Univ. and Lock Haven Univ... His hobby is music... His wife is Erin...

Awards: Most Technical Wrestler at 1999 Cerro Pelado Tournament in Cuba... Outstanding Wrestler at 1989 Cadet World Championships and 1989 Cadet Nationals.

LINCOLN McILRAVY

2000-01 Team USA Ranking: Ranked 1st at 69 kg/152 lb

Years on Team USA: 5 (1996-00)

Residence: Coralville, IA

Club: Gateway WC

College: Univ. of Iowa

High School: Philip, SD

Born: July 17, 1974, in Rapid City, SD

Height: 5' 8"

International Competition: Third in 2000 Dan Kolav Tournament (Bulgaria)... Second in 1999 World Championships... 1999 Pan American Games champion... 1998-00 World Cup champion... 1999 Poland Open champion... Third in 1998 World Championships... 1998 Goodwill Games champion... 1998 Yarygin Tournament champion (Russia)... Member of 1997 U.S. World Team... 1996 Sunkist International Open champion... Third in 1996 Yarygin Tournament (Russia)... Second in 1995 Sunkist/ASU International Open... 1995 Trophe Milone Tournament champion (Italy)... Member of Junior World Team

U.S. Competition: 1997-2000 U.S. Nationals champion... 1997-99 World Team Trials champion... Third in 1996 U.S. Olympic Team Trials... Second in 1996 U.S. Nationals... 1995

NYAC Christmas Open champion... Seventh in 1995 U.S. Nationals... 1995 Northern Plains Regional champion... 1990 Cadet Nationals champion... 1991 Junior Nationals champion... 1990 Cadet Nationals champion...

College: 1993-94 and 1997 NCAA champion for the Univ. of Iowa, coached by Dan Gable... 1995 NCAA runner-up... Took a redshirt year in 1995-96 to pursue Olympics... Majored in physical therapy...

High School: Five-time South Dakota state champion for Philip HS, coached by Dan Mahoney (1988-92)...

Personal: He and his wife, Lisa, have two young boys, Streeter and Sterling... Hobbies including wood working, motorcycling and skiing... Works as an assistant wrestling coach at the Univ. of Iowa... Involved in Fellowship of Christian Athletes and Athletes in Action.

BRANDON SLAY

2000-01 Team USA Ranking: Ranked 1st at 76kg/167.5 lb

Years on Team USA: 1 (2000)

Residence: Colorado Springs, CO

Club: Dave Schultz WC

College: Univ. of Pennsylvania

High School: Amarillo, TX (Tascosa HS)

Born: October 14, 1975, in Amarillo, TX

Height: 5' 8"

International Competition: Second in 2000 Dave Schultz Memorial International... Second in 1999 Henri Deglane Challenge (France)... 1999 Dan Kolov Tournament champion (Bulgaria)... Second in 1999 Poland Open... 1999 Dave Schultz Memorial International champion... 1998 Five Continents Cup champion (Australia)... Third in 1998 Sunkist Kids International Open... Fourth in 1997 Sunkist Kids International Open... Fifth in 1997 Pearl of Macedonia... 1995 Pan Pacific Games champion... Fifth in 1992 Junior World Championships in freestyle... Second in 1991 Cadet World Championships in Greco-Roman... Third in 1990 Cadet World Championships in Greco-Roman...

U.S. Competition: 2000 U.S. Nationals Champion... Sixth in the 1999 World Team Trials... Competed in the 1999 U.S. Nationals... 1996 and 1999 University Nationals champion... Third in 1998 Winter Classic... Third in 1998 University Nationals... 1995 Espoir Nationals champion in both styles... Second in 1993 Junior Nationals in Greco-Roman... Fourth in 1992 Junior Nationals in both styles... Fifth in 1991 Junior Nationals in Greco-Roman... 1990 Cadet Nationals champion in Greco-Roman... Sixth in 1990 Cadet Nationals...

College: Attended the Univ. of Pennsylvania, coached by Roger Reina... Second in 1997 and 1998 NCAA Championships... Received a degree in finance and management from the Wharton School of Business in 1998.

High School: Attended Tascosa High School, where he was coached by Johnny Cobb... Three-time Texas high school champion (1991-93), and placed second in 1990... Named all-district in football two times, and was named Texas Panhandle Defensive player of the year in 1992...

Personal: U.S. Olympic Training Center resident athlete... Hobbies are watching movies, waterskiing and skiing... He is an investment specialist with the Charles Schwab Corporation.

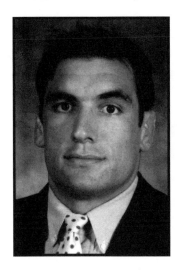

CHARLES BURTON

2000-2001 Team USA Ranking: No. 1 at 85 kg/187.25 lb

Years on Team USA: 2 (1999-01)

Residence: Bloomington, IN

Club: New York AC

College: Boise State Univ.

High School: Meridian, ID (Centennial)

Born: October 9, 1973, in Ontario, OR

Height: 5' 8"

International Competition: 2000 Takhti Cup (Iran) Champion... Second in 2000 Dan Kolav Tournament (Bulgaria)... Fourth in 1998 and 1999 Sunkist Kids International Open... Fourth in 1999 Dave Schultz Memorial International... Third in 1998 Colorado International Open... Third in 1997 Pan American Championships...

U.S. Competition: 2000 U.S. Olympic Special Wrestle-off champion... 2000 U.S. Olympic Team Trials champion... Second in 2000 U.S. Nationals... 1999 New York AC Christmas Open Champion... Second in 1999 World Team Trials... Third in 1999 U.S. Nationals... 1997 Winter Classic champion... Seventh in 1997 U.S. Nationals... 1997 University Nationals champion... Third in 1993 Espoir Nationals...

College: Competed for Boise State Univ., coached by Mike Young... Third in 1996 NCAA Championships... Studied secondary education and physical education...

High School: Competed for Centennial High School in Meridian, Idaho... 1991 State Champion...

Personal: Works as an assistant wrestling coach at Indiana Univ... Served as an assistant wrestling coach at Boise State and Iowa State in 1996-97 season... He enjoys fly-fishing, backpacking, and hunting.

MELVIN DOUGLAS

2000-01 Team USA Ranking: Ranked 1st at 97 kg/213.75 lb

Years on Team USA: 11 (1988-90, 1991-00)

Residence: Mesa, AZ

Club: Sunkist Kids

College: Univ. of Oklahoma

High School: Topeka, KS (Highland Park HS)

Born: August 21, 1963, in Topeka, KS

Height: 5' 9"

International Competition: 2000 Olympic Qualifier champion (Mexico)... Third in 2000 Cerro Pelado Tournament (Cuba)... 1995 and 1999 Sunkist International Open champion... Fifth in 1998 World Championships... Second in 1998 Goodwill Games... Second in 1998 Takhti Cup (Iran)... Ninth in 1997 World Championships... 1997 Yasar Dogu Tournament champion (Turkey)... Seventh in 1996 Olympic Games... Third in 1994-95 World Championships... 1995 Pan American Games champion... 1995 Cerro Pelado Tournament champion... 1995 Michigan International Open champion... Second in 1994 Goodwill Games... 1994 World Cup champion... 1994 Cerro Pelado champion (Cuba)... 1993 World champion...1992-93 U.S. Open Grand Prix champion...

Third in 1993 Krasnoyarsk Tournament (Russia)... 1992 Cerro Pelado Tournament champion (Cuba)... 1992 Sunkist International Duals champion... 1991 Sunkist International Open runner-up... 1991 President's Cup champion (Turkey)... 1990 U.S. Open International champion... Third in the 1990 World Cup... 1989 World silver medalist... 1989 Tbilisi Tournament champion (Soviet Union)... 1988 Sunkist International Open champion... 1986 Hall of Fame Classic champion...

U.S. Competition: Eight-time U.S. Nationals champion (1988, 1993-98, 2000)... 1993-95 and 1997-98 World Team Trials champion... 1996 U.S. Olympic Team Trials champion... 1992 Olympic Team Trials runner-up at 180.5 pounds... Second in the 1987, 1991-92 U.S. Nationals... 1991 World Team Trials runner-up... Fourth in 1990 World Team Trials... 1989 U.S. Olympic Festival champion... 1988 Olympic Trials runner-up...Third in 1987 U.S. Olympic Festival... Sixth in the 1986 U.S. Nationals... 1981 Junior National champion...

College: Competed for Stan Abel at Univ. of Oklahoma... 1985 & 1986 NCAA champion as a junior and senior... Graduated in 1986 with degree in art advertising...

High School: Competed for Richard Nitch at Topeka Highland Park HS in Kansas... 1979, 1980 & 1981 state champion as a sophomore, junior, and senior...

Personal: He and his wife,Theresa, have three children, Christina, Melvin IV, and Isaiah... Brothers Larry and Terry were high school state wrestling champions... Works for Home Depot...

Awards: 1998 Common Ground Award for Sports winner, recognizing international diplomacy through sport... 1994 USA Wrestling Freestyle Wrestler of the Year... 1994 USA Wrestling Athlete of the Year... 1994 Championship Belt Series winner.

KERRY McCOY

2000-01 Team USA Ranking: Ranked 1st at 130 kg/286 lb

Years on Team USA: 5 (1994-95, 96-97, 98-00)

Residence: State College, PA

Club: New York AC

College: Penn State Univ.

High School: Longwood, NY

Born: August 2, 1974, in Riverhead, NY

Height: 6' 2"

International Competition: 1993 and 2000 Pan American Championships champion... 1999 and 2000 World Cup champion... Third in 1999 Yasar Dogu Tournament (Turkey)... Fourth in 1998 World Championships... Second in 1998 Goodwill Games... 1998 Cerro Pelado Tournament champion (Cuba)... 1997 Uzbekistan Cup champion... 1997 Sunkist Kids International Open champion... Third in 1996 Cerro Pelado Tournament (Cuba)... Second in 1996 Michigan International Open... Third in 1993-95 Sunkist International Open... Second in 1994 U.S. Open International... Seventh in 1993 Espoir World Championships in Greco-Roman... 1992 Junior World Champion... Second in 1990 Cadet World Championships...

U.S. Competition: 2000 U.S. Nationals champion... Second in 1999 World Team Trials... 1997-98 and 2000 New York AC Christmas Open champion... 1998 World Team Trials champion... Fifth in 1998 U.S. Nationals... Fourth in 1995 and 1997 World Team Trials... Second in 1996-97 U.S. Nationals... Third in 1996 U.S. Olympic Team Trials... Third in 1994 World Team Trials... Fourth in 1994 U.S. Nationals... Second in 1993 Espoir Nationals... 1993 Espoir Nationals champion in Greco-Roman... 1993 University Nationals champion... Fourth in 1992 Espoir Nationals... Third in 1992 Junior Nationals... Second in 1990 Cadet Nationals...

College: Attended Penn State Univ., coached by John Fritz and Hachiro Oishi... 1994 and 1997 NCAA heavyweight champion... Third in the 1995 NCAA Championships as a junior... Took a redshirt year in 1995-96 to pursue Olympics... He studied marketing...

High School: Competed for Mike Piccozzi at Longwood HS in New York... 1992 state champion as a senior... Second in 1991 state meet as a junior... Asics Tiger All-American First Team member... Served as senior class president and played cello in the orchestra...

Personal: Works as an assistant wrestling coach at Penn State... Served as Chairperson for the NCAA Student-Athlete Advisory Committee... Served as President, Student Athlete Advisory Board (Penn State Univ.)... Volunteer for community outreach program... Hobbies include playing tennis, music, cello, and television.

Greco-Roman

STEVEN MAYS

2000-01 Team USA Ranking: No. 1 at 54 kg/119 lb

Years on Team USA: 5 (1995-97, 98-01)

Residence: Pensacola, FL

Club: U.S. Navy

College: None

High School: Kalamazoo, MI (Gull Lake HS)

Born: June 17, 1966, in Kalamazoo, MI

Height: 5' 5"

International Competition: Fifth in 2000 Colo. Spgs. Olympic qualifier... DNP in 1999 World Championships... Third in 1999 Pan American Games... Second in 1999 Nordvest Cup (Norway)... Eighth in 1997 Granma Cup (Cuba)... Third in 1995 Sunkist International Open...

U.S. Competition: 2000 U.S. Olympic Team Trials Champion... Second in 1996 and 2000 U.S. Nationals... Second in 2000 Armed Forces Championships... 1999 World Team Trials champion... 1999 U.S. Nationals champion... Five-time Armed Forces champion (1989, 1992-93, 1999)... Third in 1998 World Team Trials... Third in 1998 U.S. Nationals... Fourth in 1998 Armed Forces Championships... Third in

1996-97 Armed Forces Championships... Second in 1996 U.S. Olympic Team Trials... Third in 1995 World Team Trials... Eighth in 1995 U.S. Nationals... Second in 1991, 1994 & 2000 Armed Forces... Sixth in 1992 U.S. Nationals... Fifth in 1992 Olympic Team Trials... Fifth in 1991 World Team Trials... Fourth in 1987 U.S. Nationals...

High School: Second in 1984 Michigan state meet for Gull Lake HS...

Personal: He is an aviation boatswain mate in the U.S. Navy... His wife is Melanie. They have three children: Danyiel, Dacia, and Aailyah.

JIM GRUENWALD

2000-01 Team USA ranking: No. 1 at 58 kg/127.75 lb

Years on Team USA: 5 (1994-95, 1997-01)

Residence: Colorado Springs, CO

Club: Sunkist Kids

College: Maranatha Baptist Bible College

High School: Greendale, WI

Born: June 9, 1970, in Milwaukee, WI

Height: 5' 4"

International Competition: 2000 Olympic Qualifier (Egypt) champion... Ninth in 2000 Olympic Qualifier (Uzbekistan)... Third in 2000 Olympic Qualifier (France)... Third in 2000 Olympic Qualifier (Italy)... 1999 Winter Classic champion...

1998-99 Sunkist Kids International Open champion... 1999 Poland Open champion... Fifth in 1999 Granma Cup (Cuba)... 1999 Dave Schultz Memorial International champion... Third in 1998 Henri Deglane Challenge (France)... 1998 Concord Cup champion... 1998 Pan American Championships champion... 1998 Sweden Cup Grand Prix champion... Second in 1998 Peer Gynt Cup (Norway)... Second in 1997 Pan-Am Games... Second in 1997 Concord Cup... Second in 1996 Sunkist International Open... Fourth in 1996 Greco-Roman World Cup... Seventh in 1996 Poddubny Tournament (Russia)... Third in 1995 Sunkist International Open... Third in 1995 Concord Cup... Fourth in 1995 Peer Gynt Cup (Norway)... Fourth in 1994 Concord Cup...

U.S. competition: 2000 U.S. Olympic Team Trials Champion... 1998-99 Winter Classic champion... Second in U.S. Nationals five times (1996-00)... Second in 1997-99 World Team Trials... Fourth in 1996 U.S. Olympic Team Trials... 1996 West Regional Olympic Trials champion... Fifth in 1995 U.S. Nationals... Second in 1994 Winter Classic... Second in 1994 U.S. Olympic Festival... Third in 1994 World Team Trials... Fourth in 1994 U.S. Nationals... Third in 1993-94 University Nationals... 1994 Rocky Mountain Regional champion... 1993 U.S. Olympic Festival champion... Second in 1988 Junior Nationals... Third in 1987 Junior Nationals... 1986 Cadet Nationals champion...

College: Competed for Ben Peterson, the 1972 Olympic champion, at Maranatha Baptist Bible College... Three-time National Christian College champion, winning titles in 1989, 1991 and 1992, finished second in 1990... Graduated in 1994 with a degree in secondary education...

High School: Competed for Rob Carlson at Greendale HS in Wisconsin... He won the 1987 state title as a junior... Second in 1986 and 1988 state meets...

Personal: U.S. Olympic Training Center Resident Athlete... Works as a math teacher at Hilltop Baptist HS... His wife's name is Rachel, also a teacher at Hilltop Baptist HS... Hobbies include reading and weightlifting... Volunteers as a wrestling referee...

Awards: Who's Who of American High School Students... Who's Who of American College Students... Who's Who of American Teachers.

KEVIN BRACKEN

2000-01 Team USA Ranking: Ranked 1st at 63 kg/138.75 lb

Years on Team USA: 5 (1996-00)

Residence: Colorado Springs, CO

Club: New York AC

College: Illinois State Univ.

High School: Chicago, IL (St. Lawrence HS)

Born: October 29, 1971, in Chicago, IL

Height: 5' 6"

International Competition: Second in 2000 Granma Cup (Cuba)... Seventh in 2000 Olympic Qualifier (France)... Second in 2000 Dave Schultz Memorial International... Second in 1999 Sunkist Kids International Open... Third in 1999 Poland Open... Ninth in 1999 Granma Cup (Cuba)... Fifth in 1999 Dave Schultz Memorial International... 1998 Sunkist Kids International Open champion...Competed in the 1998 World Championships...Sixth in 1998 Concord Cup...

Second in 1997-98 Pan American Championships... Fourth in 1998 Vehbi Emri Tournament (Turkey)...Fifth in 1996-97 Granma Cup (Cuba)...1996 World Cup champion... Second in 1996 Michigan International Open... Second in 1995 Haparanda Cup (Sweden)...Sixth in 1995 Sunkist International Open...Third in 1993 Pan American Championships...1992 Michigan WC Invitational champion...

U.S. Competition: 2000 U.S. Nationals champion... Third in 1999 World Team Trials... Second in 1998-99 U.S. Nationals... 1999 NYAC Greco-Roman champion... 1998 Winter Classic champion... Second in 1997-98 World Team Trials... 1997 U.S. Nationals champion... Third in 1996 U.S. Olympic Team Trials... Third in 1996 U.S. Nationals... 1996 North Regional Olympic Trials champion... Fourth in 1995 World Team Trials... 1995 U.S. Olympic Festival champion... Fourth in 1992-93 and 1995 U.S. Nationals... 1993 and 1995 University Nationals champion... Fourth in 1993 World Team Trials... Third in 1992 Olympic Team Trials... Second in 1992 Michigan WC Open... Eighth in 1992 Concord Cup... Second in 1991 Espoir Nationals... 1990 Junior Nationals champion... Second in 1989 Junior Nationals...

College: Competed for coach Kevin Bellis at Illinois State Univ., where he received a bachelor's degree in physical education... Three-time NCAA tournament qualifier...

High School: Competed for Tom Gauger at St. Lawrence HS in Illinois, where he placed third in the 1990 state championships... He was also an honorable mention all-state football player, and a conference champion pole vaulter...

Personal: U.S. Olympic Training Center resident athlete... Previously worked as an assistant wrestling coach at the Univ. of Northern Illinois... His hobbies are biking, fishing, and hiking... Speaks to area schools and youth clubs on a regular basis...

Awards: Outstanding Wrestler at 1998 Sunkist Kids International Open... Outstanding Wrestler at 1998 Colorado Open... 1994 Illinois State Univ. Male Athlete of the Year.

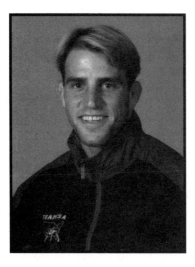

HEATH SIMS

2000-01 Team USA Ranking: Ranked 1st at 69 kg/152 lb

Years on Team USA: 5 (1990-91, 93-96, 98-00)

Residence: Huntington Beach, CA

Club: Dave Schultz WC

High School: Woodbridge, CA

Born: October 14, 1971 in Orange, CA

Height: 5' 8"

International Competition: 2000 Pan American Olympic Qualifying Challenge champion... Third in 2000 Pan American Championships... 2000 Dave Schultz Memorial International champion... Fourth in 1999 Sunkist Kids International Open (76 kg)... Fourth in 1998 Henri Deglane Challenge (France)... 1998 Sunkist Kids International Open champion... Second in 1997 Sunkist Kids International Open... Fourth in 1995 World Cup... 1995 U.S. World team member... Fourth in 1995 Concord Cup... Fifth in 1995 Peer Gynt Cup (Norway)... Fifth in 1994 Concord Cup... Second in 1994 Spring Cup (Israel)... Second in 1994 Petrov Cup (Bulgaria)... Fourth in 1993 World Cup... Fourth in 1993 Concord Cup... Second in 1991 Espoir World Championships... Fourth in 1991 Granma Cup (Cuba)...

U.S. Competition: 1995 and 2000 U.S. Nationals champion... 2000 West Olympic Regional Trials champion... Sixth in 1999 World Team Trials... Third in 1998 World Team Trials... Sixth in 1998 U.S. Nationals... Fourth in 1996 U.S. Olympic Team Trials... Fourth in 1996 U.S. Nationals... 1996 West Regional Olympic Trials champion... 1995 World Team Trials champion... 1995 University Nationals champion... Second in 1994 U.S. Olympic Festival... Second in 1990 and 1993-94 World Team Trials... Third in 1993-94 U.S. Nationals... 1990 and 1994 University Nationals champion... 1990 and 1993 U.S. Olympic Festival champion... Second in 1993 University Nationals... Fourth in 1991 World Team Trials... Seventh in 1990-91 U.S. Nationals... Fourth in 1991 University Nationals... 1989-91 Espoir Nationals champion... Second in 1988-89 Junior Nationals...

College: Attended Pikes Peak Community College in Colorado Springs, Colo... Attended Arizona State Univ. for one semester...

High School: Competed for Cliff Nelson at Woodbridge HS in California... 1988 and 1989 California state champion...

Personal: Hobbies include surfing, mountain biking, and sky diving... He has a daughter, Skye...

Awards: Outstanding Greco-Roman Wrestler at 2000 Dave Schultz Memorial International... Outstanding Greco-Roman Wrestler at 1995 University Nationals... Outstanding Greco-Roman Wrestler at 1990 Espoir Nationals.

MATT LINDLAND

2000-01 Team USA Ranking: Ranked 1st at 76 kg/167.5 lb

Years on Team USA: 7 (1994-00)

Residence: Lincoln, NE

Club: Sunkist Kids

College: Univ. of Nebraska

High School: Gladstone, OR

Born: May 17, 1970, in Oregon City, OR

Height: 6' 0"

International Competition: 2000 Pan American Championships champion... 2000 Olympic Qualifier champion (Egypt)... Third in 2000 Olympic Qualifier (Uzbekistan)... DNP at 1999 World Championships... 1999 Pan American Games champion... Second in 1998-99 Granma Cup (Cuba)... Fourth in 1999 Dave Schultz Memorial International... Sixth in 1998 World Championships... Second in 1998 Concord Cup... Third in 1998 Vehbi Emri Tournament (Turkey)... Third in 1997 Sunkist Kids International Open... 1997 U.S. World Team member... 1997 Pytlasinki Grand Prix champion (Poland)... Second in 1997 Pan American Championships... Fifth in 1996-97 Granma Cup (Cuba)... 1996 World Cup champion... 1996 Sunkist Kids International Open champion... Second in 1996 Poland Open... Second in 1996 Vehbi Emre Tournament (Turkey)... Fourth in 1995 Karelin Cup (Russia)... Second in 1995 World Cup... 1994 Pan American Championships titlist in freestyle... Fifth in 1993 Concord Cup...

U.S. Competition: 1995 and 1998-99 and 2000 U.S. Nationals champion... Second in 2000 West Olympic Regional Trials... 1997-99 World Team Trials champion... Second in 1996-97 U.S. Nationals... Third in 1996 U.S. Olympic Team Trials... Second in 1995 World Team Trials... Third in 1994 Winter Classic... 1994 U.S. Olympic Festival champion... Second in 1994 U.S. Olympic Festival in freestyle... Third in 1994 World Team Trials... Sixth in 1994 U.S. Nationals... 1992 & 1994 University Nationals champion in freestyle... Seventh in 1993 U.S. Nationals... Third in 1993 University Nationals... Fourth in 1992 University Nationals... 1992 Southern Olympic Regional Trials champion... Second in 1991 University Nationals... Third in 1990 U.S. Olympic Festival... Second in 1990 Espoir Nationals... Seventh in 1987 Junior Nationals...

College: Competed two years for Tim Neumann at the Univ. of Nebraska... Competed two years for Jim Jackson and Mike Haluska at Clackamas Community College... 1991 National Junior College Athletic Association (NJCAA) champion...

High School: Competed for Rich Holloman at Gladstone HS in Oregon... Second in 1989 state meet as a senior... Third in 1988 state tournament as a junior...

Personal: He and his wife, Angie, have a son, James, and a daughter, Robin... Works as coach of the Husker Wrestling Club at the Univ. of Nebraska... Participated in equestrian as a youth... Has participated as a speaker with the D.A.R.E. program... His hobby is spending time with his family...

Awards: 1998 USA Wrestling Greco-Roman Wrestler of the Year.

QUINCEY CLARK

2000-01 Team USA Ranking: Ranked 1st at 85 kg/187.25 lb

Years on Team USA: 4 (1997-00)

Residence: New Brighton, MN

Club: Minnesota Storm

College: Univ. of Oklahoma

High School: San Diego, CA (Lincoln Prep HS)

Born: June 5, 1972, in Norman, OK

Height: 5' 11 1/2"

International Competition: Second in 2000 Granma Cup (Cuba)... Eighth in 1999 World Championships... Second in 1999 Pan American Games... Seventh in 1999 Poland Open... Second in 1999 Sweden Cup... Second in 1999 Nordvest Cup (Norway)... Ninth in 1998 World Championships... Third in 1998 Concord Cup... Fourth in 1998 Sweden Cup Grand Prix... Second in 1998 Peer Gynt Cup (Norway)... Fifth in 1997 Sunkist Kids International Open... 1997 Michigan International Open champion... Member of 1991 Espoir World Team...

U.S. Competition: 1999 and 2000 U.S. Nationals champion... 2000 Northern Plains Regionals champion... 1998-99 World Team Trials champion... 1997-99 Northern Plains Regional champion... Sixth in 1997-98 U.S. Nationals... Third in 1997 Winter Classic... Third in 1997 World Team Trials... Second in 1996 University Nationals... Second in 1991 Espoir Nationals...

College: Attended the Univ. of Oklahoma, coached by Jack Spates... Second in 1996 NCAA Championships... Also attended San Diego State, coached by Roye Oliver, where he was seventh in the 1992 NCAA Championships... He majored in accounting...

High School: Attended Lincoln Prep HS, where he was coached by Willy Jones... Also lettered in football...

Personal: His hobbies are piano, trumpet, judo, jiu jitsu, and Bible study.

GARRETT LOWNEY

2000-01 Team USA Ranking: No. 1 at 97 kg/213.75 lb

Years on Team USA: 1 (2000-01)

Residence: Minneapolis, MN

Club: Minnesota Storm

College: Univ. of Minnesota

High School: Appleton, WI (Freedom HS)

Born: October 3, 1979, in Freedom, WI

Height: 5' 11"

International Competition: Fourth in 2000 Sweden Cup... Third in 2000 Dave Schultz Memorial International... Second in 1999 Sunkist Kids International Open... 1999 FILA Junior Greco-Roman World Champion...

U.S. Competition: 2000 U.S. Olympic Team Trials Champion... Second in 2000 U.S. Nationals... 1999 University Nationals Greco-Roman champion... 1998 Junior National Greco-Roman and freestyle champion... 1997 Junior National Greco-Roman and freestyle champion... 1996 Junior National Greco-Roman champion...

College: Competes for J. Robinson at the University of Minnesota...

High School: Competed for Freedom HS in Appleton, WI....
Three-time Wisconsin state champion... Compiled a 155-55
career record with 97 pins... Asics Tiger First-Team All-
American...

Awards: Winner of the National Wrestling Hall of Fame Dave
Schultz High School Excellence Award.

RULON GARDNER

2000-01 Team USA Ranking:
Ranked 1st at 130 kg/286 lb

Years on Team USA: 5 (1995-
96, 97-00)

Residence: Colorado Springs,
CO

Club: Sunkist Kids

College: Univ. of Nebraska

High School: Afton, WY (Star
Valley HS)

Born: Aug. 16, 1971 in Afton,
WY

Height: 6' 3"

International Competition: 1998 and 2000 Pan American
Championships champion... 2000 Gramma Cup (Cuba)
champion... 1999 Winter Classic champion... 1999 Sunkist
Kids International Open champion... 1999 Poland Open
champion... Third in 1999 Granma Cup (Cuba)... 1999 and
2000 Dave Schultz Memorial International champion... 1998
Vaanta Cup champion (Finland)... 1996-98 Sunkist Kids
International Open champion... 1998 Concord Cup
champion... Third in 1998 Tropheo Milone (Italy)... 1998
Hungary Grand Prix champion... 1995 and 1998 Granma Cup

champion (Cuba)... 1998 Colorado International Open champion... Fifth in 1997 World Championships... 1997 Pytlasinski Grand Prix champion (Poland)... Second in 1997 Pan American Championships... Second in 1997 Concord Cup... Second in 1997 Granma Cup (Cuba)... Ninth in 1997 Poddubny Tournament (Russia)... 1996 World Cup champion... 1996 Michigan International Open champion... Second in 1995 Sunkist International Open... Second in 1995 Concord Cup... Third in 1994 Sunkist International Open... Third in 1994 Ocean State International in freestyle... 1994 Pan American Championships titlist in freestyle...

U.S. Competition: 1995, 1997 and 2000 U.S. Nationals champion... Third in 1999 World Team Trials... Second in 1994 and 1998-99 U.S. Nationals... 1998 Winter Classic champion... Third in 1998 World Team Trials... 1997 World Team Trials champion... 1995, 1997 and 2000 U.S. Nationals champion... Third in 1996 U.S. Nationals... Second in 1995 World Team Trials... 1995 University Nationals champion in both styles... Second in 1994 U.S. Olympic Festival... Fifth in 1993-94 U.S. Nationals in freestyle... 1994 University Nationals freestyle champion...

College: Competed for Tim Neumann at Univ. of Nebraska... Fourth in 1993 NCAA Championships for Univ. of Nebraska... Received a degree in physical education in 1996... 1991 NJCAA champion for Ricks College and third in 1990 NJCAA Nationals, where he was coached by Bob Christensen...

High School: Competed for Kevin Kennington at Star Valley HS in Wyoming... 1989 state high school champion... He was also all-state in football, and second in the state in shot put...

Personal: His hobbies are rollerblading and relaxing... His wife is Stacy... U.S. Olympic Training Center resident athlete... His brother Reynold wrestled for Oregon State University... He was ranked sixth in freestyle in 1994-95...

Awards: 1999 Sunkist Kids International Open Greco-Roman Outstanding Wrestler... 1997-98 Greco-Roman Championship Belt Series winner... 1997 USA Wrestling Greco-Roman Wrestler of the Year... 1997 USOC Greco-Roman Wrestler of the Year.

3

The 7 Basic Skills

Every sport has certain "basics" that are used to build the foundation for more advanced techniques and strategies. When you begin the sport of wrestling, there are six fundamental skills to learn and practice—and one more after you've gained experience—before that important first bout. These seven basic skills are the stance; motion; changing levels; penetration; the lift; the backstep; and the back arch. Since each skill builds on the first one, it is important to learn and practice them in order.

A T-shirt, shorts, socks, and wrestling shoes are all you need for practice, by the way. (See Chapter 4, "The Match," for more detailed descriptions of competition clothes.)

The Seven Skills

Stance is the correct position needed for balance and the first skill to learn. It is from this starting point that you will make subsequent moves to attack your opponent. Position requires balance, so your weight should be distributed equally on both feet, your head should be up, and your eyes looking straight ahead. But there's a bit more, because this sport engages your entire body. Spread your feet as wide as your shoulders, with your knees bent at an angle and your hips flexed, set, and square. Roll your back slightly with your shoulders in and over your knees. Tuck your elbows in close to your body so they are inside your knees, and keep your forearms inside. With your weight slightly forward, hold your hands out in front of your hips—palms forward and your fingers up.

Position staggered, front view

Motion follows from your stance or position. Moving to and from your opponent depends largely on the smooth motion of your hands, arms, legs, and feet and less on strength. In

USA Wrestling

Position square, side view

the correct stance, or position, the wrestler takes short, shuffling steps and moves laterally or in a circle. This keeps his muscles flexed and ready. The wrestler never moves backward or crosses his feet. He keeps his feet spread for balance so that he can slide smoothly against his opponent.

A good way to practice motion is by getting a partner who

is your size and, literally, putting your heads together! Get into the stance position, but with your foreheads touching. Then move smoothly to the right and left, while maintaining position.

Changing levels is one of the difficult basic skills because the wrestler has to use this technique to respond to his opponent's body moves and then react by changing his own body moves. So be patient with yourself on this one. To change levels, start with your knees bent and your back straight. Don't bend at the waist, but think of your hips as an elevator that

USA Wrestling

Motion No. 1

moves up and down vertically. Keep your head up—don't bob or nod—and try to stay on the same level as your opponent. Remember, he has learned these same basic skills, too, and can be your mirror.

Level change No. 1

Penetration is one of the most important skills; combined with the first three basics, it teaches you how to break your opponent's position. (Remember, that your opponent is trying to do the same thing to you.) Keep your hands moving and try to get them inside your opponent's hands. This is *inside control*—a definite advantage because it often allows you to break the position of your opponent by doing one of three things. If your opponent's hands are too high, with inside control you can push your opponent's wrists up by forming a yoke between the thumb and forefinger of your hand. If your opponent's hands are too low, you can slap his hands down and force him to break his position. Finally, from your inside control position, you can use one forearm—keep your elbows tucked in—to push his hands apart. These three methods take your opponent out of his position and allow you to penetrate.

USA Wrestling

Level change No. 2

Changing your level (basic skill number three) is another way to get your opponent to break position. Bend at the knees, lower your body, and take a half step in with the foot you are driving off of. Then penetrate by taking a deep step inside your opponent's front foot. An alternative method is to bend at the knees, lower your body, and take a half step in with your back foot. Then penetrate and drive forward and into your opponent with your other foot. Good penetration skill depends on good position, so heed a reminder from the lesson on stance: Keep your shoulders straight, your head up, your hips forward, and your feet straight. For smooth penetration, step, don't reach.

USA Wrestling

Penetration No. 2

The **lift**, skill number five, is one of the most important basic skills. To perform a lift properly, the wrestler needs the first four skills. Remember, you are building a foundation. You need to have strength to perform lifts, of course, but equally important is the position of your hips and the hips of your opponent. Legs are the key to successful lifts, for they do the work, not your back.

To begin a successful lift, kneel on one leg and have the other bent at the knee to make a 90-degree angle. Lean into your standing opponent, with your head next to his torso. Then wrap your arms around your opponent's thighs and squeeze. That secures him with your arms, while your legs complete the lifting process. Keep your head straight and under your opponent's arm. (His elbow will be just behind your ear.)

Keep your back straight and vertical and your hips lower than his. Then use the power of your legs to complete the lift.

One way to build strength in your legs is to practice doing squats with a partner on your shoulders. Five squats are

Lift No. 1

enough to start with; then switch positions with your partner. Do one or two squats if that is what's comfortable for you in the beginning. As with any conditioning or strength-building exercise, don't overdo.

USA Wrestling

Lift No. 2

A **backstep** enables you to get into position so you can lift your opponent. This skill requires rotating your hips into and under your opponent, so he ends up behind you and over your hips. Keep your feet close together, so your support point is small. Once you're in position, do a level change, then rotate your hips "to and through" your opponent.

USA Wrestling

Backstep No. 3

The **back arch** is the move used to perform the incredible lifts and throws seen at the higher levels of wrestling. Therefore, it is not a skill you will learn until you've had a lot of practice and experience with the first six skills! Let your coach decide when you are ready for the back arch.

USA Wrestling

Back arch No. 1

With practice, you will develop "muscle memory" and should be able to perform the seven basic skills almost without thinking.

4

The Match

Wrestling is a year-round indoor sport that doesn't depend on the weather, nor does it require a substantial investment in uniforms or accessories. This makes it one of the more affordable sports for a family. By now you may have learned the basics or had some experience wrestling at school or with a wrestling club. But you probably haven't competed in a match where your opponents may be perfect strangers. Here is what to expect.

Behind the Scenes

Every successful wrestling competition needs several people working behind the scenes to ensure that the competition runs smoothly. On the local level, volunteers—moms, dads, brothers, sisters, and friends—handle many of the arrangements for setting up a competition, so wrestling can be a family and community event. At the higher levels of competition, *i.e.*, National, World, and Olympic Games competitions, highly trained and certified FILA and USA Wrestling officials are in charge.

The following summary is based on the rules and regulations of FILA and/or USAW, the two official governing bodies for amateur wrestling taking place outside secondary schools and colleges. (See Chapter 6, "Scholastic and Collegiate Wrestling," for differences in equipment, clothing, mats, and scoring.)

Equipment and Clothing

Wrestling action takes place on a mat that is 9 meters in diameter, with a border 1.20-1.50 meters wide. A red, 1-meter-wide band is drawn inside the 9-meter circle and runs around the circumference. In the United States, mats used for high school and college competitions are generally used for local events.

There are some accessories used by officials, but the wrestlers need only a mat and simple gear—two singlets, shoes and socks, and, if preferred, headgear.

A one-piece **singlet** in a stretchy, body-conforming fabric, cut low in front and back, from the chest to the hips, allows easy body movement of the arms and shoulders. For competitions, you'll need two of these—one red and one blue. Singlets are available in different lengths, so check with your coaches for the style you'll need.

Shoes should be made from a lightweight, soft, flexible fabric, with high tops, good ankle support, and soles designed to grip the mat. A shoe made from a combination of leather and nylon mesh is popular. Wear cotton **socks** for their comfort and ability to absorb perspiration.

The use of shoes with heels or nailed soles, buckles, or any metallic parts is prohibited. The metal or rigid tips of shoelaces must be cut off, and the laces secured to the shoes with tape so they do not come undone during the bout. When you are not on the mat, remove your shoes.

Basic **headgear**, which is recommended for young wrestlers in scholastic competition, is made from lightweight plastic, fits over the head with a strap (or straps) between the ear protectors, and uses an adjustable strap that is secured across or under the chin. Headgear protects the ears from injury.

Lightweight knee pads may be worn, but they are not required. No jewelry may be worn, or any metallic or hard objects. Besides these basic clothing requirements and prohibitions for men and women, there are variations for women wrestlers:

A T-shirt under a man's wrestling singlet is not allowed. A leotard is required (one red and one blue, or with red or blue predominating). Wear a bra without metal fittings, such as a cotton sports bra with a T-shaped back, and use elastic or a ribbon with no metal parts to tie back your hair. All women wrestlers of all ages must wear FILA-approved ear protectors. The same jewelry prohibition for male wrestlers applies to females as well.

Before the Bout Begins

Before the weigh-in (which determines your weight competition category), a physician will check that you have no communicable diseases or skin infections. You should be clean shaven, unless you have had a beard for several months, and then it should be trimmed neatly. Short hair (or hair that is tied back) is required, and your fingernails will be checked to be sure they are short.

In most cases, after the weigh-in for international, regional, and national competitive events, numbered lots are drawn at random to determine pairings. Each wrestler draws a number from a container, and then is paired with another number, e.g., Nos. 1 and 2 make a pair; Nos. 3 and 4 are the next pair.

Officials

In general, three officials run the wrestling match: a mat chairman, a judge, and a referee. The mat chairman is the

Supreme Court and settles any disagreement between the judge and the referee. The judge awards and records the points for each wrestler's actions, based on what the referee signals and his judgment of the action or holds. The mat chairman casts the deciding vote in any disagreement between the judge and referee. The referee is in charge of the bout itself and the two wrestlers on the mat. You'll notice that officials are dressed in white shirts, pants, and shoes. Additionally, the referee wears a red and a blue cuff; the red on his left arm, the blue on his right. If you are wearing a red singlet, the points you receive are indicated by the referee raising his left arm and signaling to the judge.

When your name is called, go to the mat assigned to you. (The corner of the mat that is the same color as your singlet is where you stand.) The referee will be in the circle at the center of the mat and will call you and your opponent to his side, where he will examine both of you to see that you have no greasy cream or oil on your body and that you are not perspiring. He will check your hands and fingernails and determine that you have a handkerchief. The referee often uses a masculine French term, *Salut* (salute), to greet the two of you; you greet your opponent, shake hands with him, and start wrestling when the referee blows his whistle. The number of periods and the length of the bout vary depending on age group and gender.

The Bout and Scoring Points

The bout always begins from the stance position—which you learned about in Chapter 3. From then on, you earn points for successfully doing the following, either on offense (top position) or defense (underneath):

Pinning your opponent's shoulders to the mat for one-half second (differs for younger age groups) is what you want to achieve because that instantly makes you the victor. This move is also known as a **fall**. A **technical fall** occurs when one wrestler has a 10-point margin in the bout.

Sometimes you win by a **decision**. This happens when you score more points than your opponent. An **injury default** can also end a match when an injury prevents your opponent from continuing.

A **takedown** is taking your opponent to the mat from the standing position.

A **reversal** is when your opponent frees himself from under you and takes control.

Hand-to-hand exposure is when you turn your opponent while he has his arms outstretched.

An **escape** occurs when your opponent escapes from your control from the bottom position.

All of the above earn 1 point in international competitions.

A **high amplitude, or grand, throw** occurs when a wrestler, from the standing position, causes his opponent to lose all contact with the ground, making his opponent describe a broad sweeping curve in the air, and bringing his opponent to the ground in a direct and immediate danger position. (This throw is worth an additional 5 points, or 3 points if there is no danger.)

Exposure occurs when you are able to turn your opponent's shoulders to the mat. If you hold your opponent in this danger position for five seconds, you receive 1 extra point.

Exposure, or takedown then exposure, is a combination maneuver and earns 2 points in international competitions.

If your match is tied at the end of the period, there is a three-minute, sudden-death overtime (differs for younger age groups). Whoever scores first, wins. If neither of you scores in the time allowed, the winner is determined by the officials.

In international wrestling, if neither one of you scores at least 3 points during regulation, there is a three-minute overtime (differs for younger age groups). Whoever gets 3 points first is the winner. If neither one of you does, the winner is determined by the officials.

Naturally, there are penalties when the rules are broken, as there are in any sport. Penalties earn points, but not the kind you want, because your penalty points are awarded to your opponent.

An **illegal hold without consequence** will cost you 1 point, plus you are cautioned. A **caution** from the referee means an infraction of the rules has occurred.

An **illegal hold with consequence** is 2 points, plus a caution.

If you **flee the mat**, that is 1 or 2 points, plus a caution. A wrestler flees the mat when he is standing or in the *par terre* position (on the ground) and is obviously avoiding his opponent.

If you **flee the hold**, that is 1 point, plus a caution. Fleeing the hold occurs when the wrestler obviously does not want his opponent to complete a hold.

Strictly forbidden and **illegal holds** are pulling hair, biting, pinching, pushing, strangling, or doing anything that appears to be torture or an attempt to physically hurt your opponent so you win through an injury default. All these actions are self-defeating and illegal.

Because wrestling is an active sport, it is wise to learn it that way and perform it that way. As mentioned earlier in this book, total universal wrestling is encouraged. Passivity is discouraged and means that you are not putting out enough physical effort—for example, by not initiating holds, or by holding your opponent with both hands to prevent him from wrestling. If the referee sees passive activity, he will shout that player's color, *e.g.*, Red! Red! Red! (meaning Action! Contact! Open!) and issue a passivity warning. The referee can then give the more active wrestler the option of continuing the bout in either a standing or *par terre* position.

When the Bout Ends

When the bout is over, shake hands with your opponent and wait for the official decision declaring the winner. Once the decision is announced, shake hands with the referee and your opponent's coach. These actions are important and risk a penalty if not observed by the participants involved. Finally, before you are allowed to wrestle in another bout, you must, in general, take a 30-minute break.

Wrestling match officials have their own vocabulary of terms; although the French words are rarely used in domestic U.S. competitions. A partial list follows.

International Officials' Vocabulary

A Terre—The bout is resumed in the *par terre* (literally, on the ground) position.

Action—The wrestler must execute the hold he has initiated.

Attention—The referee warns the passive wrestler before requesting a caution for refusal to assume the correct *par terre* position.

Caution—The penalty issued by the referee to a wrestler for violation of the rules.

Centre—The wrestlers must return to the center of the mat and continue the bout there.

Contact—The referee calls upon the wrestler to place both his hands on the back of his opponent, who is underneath. The wrestler in the standing position must assume "body to body" contact.

Continuer—The bout must be resumed upon this order by the the referee. The referee also uses this word to have the wrestling continued if the wrestlers stop due to confusion and look at him as if asking for an explanation.

Danger—The danger position.

Dawai—The referee encourages the wrestlers to wrestle more actively.

Declare Battu—The decision made subsequent to a defeat by obvious superiority.

Defaite—The opponent is beaten.

Disqualification—Disqualification is announced for unsportsmanlike conduct or brutality.

Fault—An illegal hold or violation of the technical rules.

Fin—The end of the bout.

Gong—The sound of the gong marks the beginning and end of a bout.

Head Up—The wrestler must raise his head. This order is given by the referee in the case of passivity and repeated attacks by a wrestler who thrusts his head forward.

Jambe—The wrestler has committed a leg error (Greco-Roman).

Non—This word is used to indicate that an action is not valid and is consequently void.

OK—The word most recognized internationally. It means the hold is legal and correct.

Open—The wrestler must alter his position and adopt more open wrestling tactics.

Out—A hold applied outside the mat.

Passif—Passive red, passive blue. The warning given to the wrestler who is passive. It is signaled by raising the arm that bears the color of the wrestler at fault.

Place—By striking the mat with his hand and at the same time pronouncing the word "place," the referee reminds the wrestlers not to flee the mat.

Salut—The wrestlers must greet each other.

Start—The invitation to the wrestlers standing at opposite corners of the mat to step to the center to be examined and to shake hands. After this, they await the referee's whistle to begin wrestling.

Stop—This word means to stop the bout.

Time Out—When one of the wrestlers stops wrestling, intentionally or because of injury or any other reason, the referee uses this expression to ask the timekeeper to stop the clock.

Touché—The word used to indicate that the wrestler is beaten by a "fall." For a fall, the referee himself says "tombé," strikes the mat with his hand, and blows his whistle to indicate the end of the bout.

Up—The bout must be resumed in the standing position.

Victory—The referee declares the winner.

Zone—This word must be used and spoken in a loud voice if the wrestlers enter the passivity zone—the 1-meter-wide band around the circumference of the mat.

Major International Competitions

In addition to the Olympic Games every four years, there are several other international wrestling competitions that take place around the world in both Greco-Roman and freestyle.

Pan American Games

At Buenos Aires, Argentina, in 1940, 16 nations met to plan the first athletic contests for the nations of the Western Hemisphere, with their goal being to improve and increase understanding through amateur athletic competition. The first Pan American Games, scheduled for 1942, were delayed by World War II and were not held until 1951. At that time, 2,000 athletes from 20 countries competed in 19 sports. By 1991, when the Games were held at Havana, Cuba, they had expanded to include 31 sports, including wrestling and judo, which follow the rules and regulations established by FILA. Every four years, one year before the Olympic Games, this contest is held, and amateur athletes from the nations of North, South, and Central America, plus the Caribbean, compete. The Games are conducted by the Pan American Sports Organization, which consists of the Olympic Games Committees from every participating country. The International Amateur Athletic Federation also cooperates in organizing and conducting the Pan American Games.

Asian Games

Organization for the Asian Games began in India after World War II, with the purpose of developing intercultural understanding and friendship in Asia. An Olympic Council of Asia (OCA) coordinates these games with its 43 member countries and regions. The first Asian Games were held at New Delhi in 1951, with 11 countries participating, and they are now held every four years. The 1994 Games were in Hiroshima, Japan; the 1998 Games were in Bangkok, Thailand. Whenever a country hosts the Games, much time and effort are spent on official exhibits of architecture, art, music, painting, and sculpture in order to promote cultural exchange, along with the athletic contests themselves.

World Cup

World Cup matches began in 1973 in Toledo, OH, with competition in freestyle wrestling only. By 1980, these matches included Greco-Roman wrestling, but competitions in the latter style were usually held in foreign countries.

World Championships

Beginning in 1961 at Yokohama, Japan, World Championships in wrestling have been held every year there are no Olympic Games. At the 1995 World Freestyle Wrestling Championship in Atlanta, GA, Kurt Angle was the first American to win a world title at 220 pounds. This 26-year-old from Pittsburgh, PA, entered the World Championships for the first time and won on his first try! Angle went on to win the gold at Atlanta in 1996 in the 100 kg (220 lb) freestyle event.

Goodwill Games

The Goodwill Games began in 1986 in Moscow and are held every four years in a Russian or American city. These games highlight the top individual wrestlers by weight class from nations around the world. So far, Americans have done well in these Games, with gold-medal performances from John Smith, Bruce Baumgartner, Dave Schultz, Zeke Jones, Townsend Saunders, and others.

5

USA Wrestling

As wrestling grew into a popular national sport, it soon became obvious that America needed one group that would serve as the umbrella organization for wrestling in the United States, as FILA had done for international wrestling since the organization was founded in Paris in 1912.

USA Wrestling (USAW)

For many years, the Amateur Athletic Union governed wrestling in the United States, but during 1968 and 1969, the U.S. Wrestling Federation was organized; by 1975 it had merged with the U.S. Kids Wrestling Federation. In 1983 the federation became USAW and was recognized by the U.S. and International Olympic Committees and FILA as the National Governing Body (NGB) for amateur wrestling in the United States.

Since 1969, when the organization held its first National Open Championships, the USAW has grown to 135,000 members, with more than 1.5 million registered athletes, and has chartered 2,600 wrestling clubs. It continues with its original objectives: Graduates of high schools and colleges can enter competitive programs; officials, coaches, and wrestlers have opportunities to gain education and develop in Greco-Roman and freestyle wrestling; and wrestlers, coaches, officials, and organizations that conduct wrestling programs have input regarding the policies and procedures that affect the sport of wrestling.

USAW works at the grassroots level to develop young wrestlers (both male and female), and trains and selects the teams that compete for the United States in national and international competitions. The group also organizes and runs regional and national championships for all wrestlers who are nine years old or older. There are camps, clinics, and educational programs for coaches, and USAW oversees the resident program for Greco-Roman wrestlers at the U.S. Olympic Training Center in Colorado Springs, CO. Here, amateur Greco-Roman wrestlers live, work, and train to improve their competitive skills.

Throughout the 1990s, USAW and FILA have cooperated in making changes to modern wrestling, as shown in the 2000 edition of the *International Rule Book & Guide to Wrestling*:

- Bouts are longer—two 3-minute periods, rather than one period of five minutes.

- "Bonus points are awarded for spectacular throws that take an opponent directly to his back. A 1-point takedown performed in spectacular fashion can become a 4-point or even a 6-point action, with a bonus for holding the opponent in bridge for five seconds."

- Clear-cut championship finals can be "scheduled at a specific time at the climax of competition."

- Rule changes make "passivity (stalling) the worst enemy of wrestling. Any attempt to avoid wrestling—by blocking, by pushing, by going out of bounds, by 'playing the edge'—is punished under a code of warnings, cautions and penalties."

Both USAW and FILA continue to promote wrestling as a sport that is active, dynamic, and "all-out."

Divisions for Younger Wrestlers

USAW has established wrestling programs at various age levels and has modified some of FILA's rules and applied them to different age and domestic competition categories.

At the scholastic level, USAW has set up age and weight categories for three divisions—Kids, Juniors, and Cadets. USAW uses modified FILA rules to accommodate these younger wrestlers who are eligible to participate at up to four levels of competition—local, regional, state, and national—depending on age. For example, Schoolgirls and Cadets wrestle for two 2-minute periods, with a 30-second break; Juniors and Seniors wrestle for two 3-minute periods with a 30-second break.

Kids Division

Schoolboy-Schoolgirl, Novice, Midget, and Bantam make up this division, each with its own weight and age categories. All members in this division are eligible to compete in local, regional, and state competitions, except those under nine years of age may not enter regional competitions. These young wrestlers are classed by age and weight, with age determined by birth date. (For example, if your birthday is in the middle of the year, you are considered that age for the entire year.) In this division, the duration of the bout and the number and length of rest periods varies depending on your category and style of wrestling.

Schoolboy-Schoolgirl (13-14 years old)

These 17 weight classes begin at 70 pounds and increase in increments of 5 pounds to 165+ pounds, with a 30-pound maximum difference. Heavyweights must weigh more than 160 pounds.

Novice (11-12 years old)

The novice category of 15 weight classes begins at 60 pounds and increases in increments of 5 pounds up to 140+ pounds, with a 25-pound maximum difference. Heavyweights must weigh more than 140 pounds.

Midget (9-10 years old)

Midgets begin at 50 pounds in 13 weight classes and increase in increments of 5 pounds up to 120+ pounds, a 20-pound maximum difference. Heavyweights must weigh more than 120 pounds.

Bantam (7-8 years old)

These lightest nine weight classes begin at 40 pounds and increase by 5 pounds for each class up to 75+ pounds, a 15-pound maximum difference. Heavyweights must weigh more than 75 pounds.

Junior Division

This division is for student-athletes attending grades 9, 10, 11, or 12 during the school term a wrestling event is held. If the event is a summer tournament, then the athlete must have attended grades 9, 10, 11, or 12 during the school term just completed. The age requirement for the Junior Division is that you must not have reached your 19th birthday prior to September 1 of your senior year. Juniors have four consecutive calendar years of eligibility, beginning with the ninth grade. Juniors are eligible for all domestic competitions in these 12 weight classes:

Junior Division Weight Classes

1. 98.0 lb	5. 132.0 lb	9. 178.0 lb
2. 105.5 lb	6. 143.0 lb	10. 191.5 lb
3. 114.5 lb	7. 154.0 lb	11. 220.0 lb
4. 123.0 lb	8. 165.0 lb	12. 220-275 lb

Cadet Division (15-16 years old)

Cadets are eligible for domestic competitions in these thirteen weight classes:

Cadet Division Weight Classes - Males

1. 83.5 lb	8. 143.0 lb
2. 88.0 lb	9. 154.0 lb
3. 94.5 lb	10. 167.0 lb
4. 103.5 lb	11. 182.5 lb
5. 112.0 lb	12. 209.0 lb
6. 121.0 lb	13. 209 to 242.0 lb
7. 132.0 lb	

Cadet Division Weight Classes - Females

1. 83.75 lb	7. 123.25 lb
2. 88.0 lb	8. 132.25 lb
3. 94.75 lb	9. 143.25 lb
4. 101.25 lb	10. 154.25 lb
5. 108 lb	11. 154.25+ lb*
6. 114.5 lb	30 lb maximum diff.

*Not a FILA weight class

In Junior, Cadet, and Kids competitions, protective headgear is required, and a face mask may be worn to protect an injury, if that is advised by a doctor. Some young wrestlers also wear knee pads and shin guards.

University Division

This division is for 18-24 year old wrestlers whose high school class has been graduated (18 year olds need a medical certificate). The nine weight classes for men range from 110 pounds to 286.5 pounds; the six weight classes for women range from 101.25 pounds to 165.25 pounds.

FILA Junior World

This category is for 18-20 year old wrestlers (17 year olds need a medical certificate). The nine weight classes for men range from 110 pounds to 286.5 pounds; the nine for women range from 88 pounds to 165.25+ pounds.

Senior (Olympic) Division

This category is for wrestlers born 1983 or before (17-19 year olds need a medical certificate). The eight weight classes range from 119 pounds to 286.5 pounds. The six weight classes for women range from 101.25 pounds to 165.25 pounds. Older wrestlers abide by FILA rules governing international competitions.

If you belong to a USAW-chartered wrestling club, or are participating in a USAW-sanctioned event at any level of competition, there are some modifications to FILA rules that you, your parents, and your coaches should be aware of:

Blood Rule (International Rule Book & Guide to Wrestling)

1. Athletes known to be infected with the HIV/HBV virus cannot compete in any USA Wrestling sanctioned event.

2. Health care attendants known to be infected with AIDS cannot administer to bleeding athletes.

3. Anytime an athlete bleeds during a bout, the action shall be stopped immediately and first aid administered.

4. A bleeding athlete cannot compete unless the bleeding and spread of blood is effectively stopped. If the spread of blood to others cannot be effectively prevented to the satisfaction of the Chief Medical Officer and officials, then the athlete cannot compete further.

5. Timeouts to stop bleeding or the spread of blood shall not be included in injury time. The cumulative time out to stop bleeding and the spread of blood shall not exceed five minutes.

6. Blood must be cleaned from the mats, uniforms and bodies with a bleach solution, and all used towels and other cleanup materials must be properly and immediately disposed of in a separate container for contaminated material.

7. Competition cannot resume until all blood has been removed and the cleaning solution residue has dried.

Other modifications have to do with weighing-in, pairing, drawing lots, and mat markings in national and international competitions. For additional information, ask your coach for details or consult a current rule book.

6

Scholastic and Collegiate Wrestling

Although wrestling has been a competitive sport for centuries, its introduction into the standard curricula at the scholastic and college level in America occurred only in the twentieth century, when junior highs, high schools, and colleges included wrestling as a competitive sport in physical education classes.

Junior High and High School Wrestling

Greco-Roman and freestyle are popular wrestling forms in America's junior high and high schools, but the most popular form is folkstyle. Folkstyle, also known as scholastic or collegiate wrestling, is a unique style practiced only in the United States. The folkstyle wrestler aims for control of his opponent while being fast and nimble on his feet, and legal holds are allowed both above and below the waist.

The mat for scholastic competitions is no more than 4 inches thick and has a diameter of 28 feet minimum, with a center circle area of 10 feet marked with parallel starting lines 1 foot apart. The lines are 1 inch wide by 3 feet long and closed at the ends by a 1-inch red or green line.

Your **singlet** will be in your school's colors and is cut higher on your torso and under the arms than those worn in national and international competitions. Full-length (but not Bermuda-length) tights are allowed. **Shoe** requirements are the same, nonslip **knee pads** may be worn, and protective **headgear** is required. If you are a member of the visiting team at a tournament, you will wear a red cuff on your left ankle when you are on the mat; the home team's wrestlers wear a green cuff.

Wrestlers are to report to the weigh-in clean shaven, with trimmed sideburns, and hair cut and under control. Your hair may not be braided, knotted, or tied, but if it is, then you must wear a cover—a water-polo cap, for example—under your headgear. (If you have a beard, then a face mask is required.) However, a small, neatly trimmed mustache is acceptable. Body coloring or marking (tattoos) and hair coloring are discouraged, since they are distractions and can be offensive to others.

Thirteen odd- and even-numbered weight classifications are designated for scholastic competitions, so no wrestler is overmatched.

Junior High and High School Weight Classes

1. 103 lb
2. 112 lb
3. 119 lb
4. 125 lb
5. 130 lb
6. 135 lb
7. 140 lb
8. 145 lb
9. 152 lb
10. 160 lb
11. 171 lb
12. 189 lb
13. 275 lb

A 215 lb class is optional.

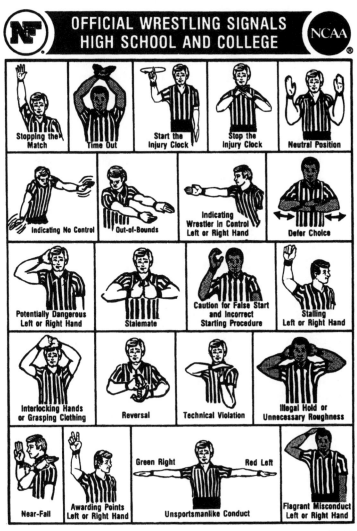

After the weigh-in, a designated member of your team will participate in a coin or disc toss to determine which odd or even weight classification will begin the match. This toss also determines who chooses the starting position (up, down, or neutral) of the wrestlers for the second period of their bout. For the third period the choice of positions is the reverse of how the wrestlers started the second period.

All wrestling matches have a common format, with a few variations. High school officials are dressed in black-and-white striped shirts, black trousers, and black shoes. They wear green and red wristbands on their right and left wrists, respectively, to match the starting lines of the home and visiting teams. Three officials are involved—the referee, timekeeper, and scorer.

Before the bouts begin, the referee supervises the weigh-in, and checks all the wrestlers to see that they are dressed properly, are well-groomed, and have no unhealthy skin conditions.

A scholastic wrestling match is 6 minutes—three 2-minute periods. There is a mandatory 45-minute rest break between bouts for each wrestler at tournaments. The first period begins with the opponents standing up and facing one another at their starting lines on the mat. The second period begins with one wrestler having a choice of top, bottom, or neutral (at least one foot on the starting line) position. Points are earned for how well holds and maneuvers are executed, and the match ends if one wrestler holds his opponent's shoulders to the mat for two seconds. If a **fall** is not achieved, a **decision** is made in favor of the wrestler with the most points. **Defaults** occur if one wrestler cannot continue the bout. A **forfeit** occurs when one wrestler does not show up for the match.

How to Score Points
Individual match points:

Near fall	2 or 3 points
Takedown	2 points
Reversal	2 points
Escape	1 point

If the match is tied at the end of regulation (6 minutes), a 2-minute overtime period follows immediately, and the wrestler scoring the first points wins. A 30-second **tiebreaker** takes place if no score is earned during the overtime period. One wrestler takes the top position with the opponent on the bottom. If the top wrestler scores or holds the bottom wrestler down, he wins. If the bottom wrestler scores, he wins. If there is still no score, the offensive, or more active and aggressive, wrestler is declared the winner.

Penalties and infractions of the rules follow the same pattern as those for national and international competitions. Potentially dangerous holds are outlawed, as are certain hammerlocks, headlocks, and strangleholds, to mention just three of the illegal holds. Wrestlers will be penalized immediately for these infractions of the rules. Furthermore, stalling—avoiding contact, refusing to wrestle aggressively, delaying tactics—are penalized and not overlooked.

At the end of the bout, you remain on the mat with your opponent and shake hands with him, while the referee declares the winner. At no time during or after the bout should you be guilty of unsportsmanlike conduct, which includes throwing your headgear or lowering the shoulder straps of your singlet. Be aware that the referee knows the difference between "throwing" and "tossing" your headgear, and keeping your singlet straps up while on the mat is pretty obvious to everyone.

For information on the National Federation of Interscholastic Coaches Association (NFICA), the National Federation of Interscholastic Officials Association (NFIOA), and complete rules and regulations governing high school wrestling in the United States, contact the National Federation of State High School Associations at:

National Federation of State High School Associations
11724 NW Plaza Circle, Box 20626
Kansas City, MO 64195-0626
Phone: (816) 464-5400

Collegiate Wrestling

The first intercollegiate wrestling match took place in the United States when the University of Pennsylvania's team met Yale's in 1900. Wrestling's popularity spread so rapidly that within four years a wrestling conference was founded among some East Coast schools.

However, it was the physical violence of college football that led to the formation of the National Collegiate Athletic Association (NCAA). One particular concern was the intense use of force in college football, especially the "flying wedge," which caused so many injuries and even deaths. The public's outcry that something had to be done to prevent violence from disrupting amateur athletics brought about a White House conference in 1905 to discuss what could be done to reform intercollegiate competition.

The regulation of collegiate wrestling was a by-product of these developments. By 1910, the NCAA's Wrestling Rules Committee had in place a set of rules to regulate wrestling matches, and over the next 20 years, the NCAA began to issue standard rules and regulations for the sport and competitions. Today, it is the official governing body for amateur wrestling in U.S. secondary schools and at the college or university level.

Although several coaches promoted wrestling at the collegiate level in the United States during the first two decades of the twentieth century, it was Edward Clark Gallagher at Oklahoma A&M (now Oklahoma State University) who made wrestling a varsity sport and built his teams into powerhouses. They suffered no defeats for 10 years, from 1922 to 1931. Every four years, many athletes competed at the Olympic Games, and this also helped to establish wrestling as an amateur sport at a collegiate level.

Collegiate Wrestling Attire

The one-piece wrestling **singlet** for collegiate competitions is cut higher in front and back and should not extend beyond the tops of your knees. You may wear full-length tights, but none that are Bermuda-length.

Your shoes should be heelless, above the ankle, and laced with eyelets. If you represent the home team, you'll wear a green cuff on your ankle; the visiting team wears a red cuff. Protective **headgear** for your ears is mandatory, and it must lock in place, so it won't come off or turn on your head, as this could cause an injury to your opponent. **Mouth guards** are recommended.

For reasons of health and safety, all wrestlers should be clean-shaven and well-groomed. Your hair should not grow below a standard shirt collar; sideburns and side hair should not grow below your earlobes. A mustache is allowed, but it must be trimmed neatly and not hang down below your lower lip.

Usually, the referee supervises the weigh-in, and you will be examined by a doctor who will determine that you are not ill with any skin infections or communicable diseases. The NCAA has adopted standard precautions for the handling of blood-borne pathogens (HBV and HIV), with some modifications that relate to athletic events. The most recent edition of the *NCAA Sports Medicine Handbook* can provide you with updated information.

The mat in collegiate wrestling has a wrestling area 32 feet in diameter, with a 5-foot apron around the wrestling area. Both these areas must be the same thickness, but not more than 4 inches. The wrestling area is marked on the mat by painted 2-inch-wide lines. A circle 10 feet in diameter is painted at the center of the mat. Within this circle are two 1-inch starting lines, 3 feet long and 10 inches apart. Two 1-inch lines close the ends of the starting lines. One of the two lines is green and is located closest to the home team; the other is red and located closest to the visiting team.

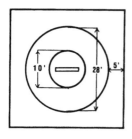

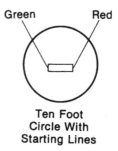

Green   Red

**Ten Foot
Circle With
Starting Lines**

National Federation of State High School Associations

High school wrestling mats

In college folkstyle wrestling, competitors are separated into ten weight classes, ranging from 118 pounds to the heavyweight class of 177-275 pounds. The NCAA established a point system to keep score during a wrestling match, and this point total, plus the time of control, is used to determine a winner when there is no **fall**. For college wrestling, the match is divided into three periods also, but is 1 minute longer than a high school bout. The first period is 3 minutes; the second and third are 2 minutes each. In general, both high school and college wrestling focus on control, and points for **takedowns** and **reversals** are awarded, as are points for **controlling** an opponent. Any **illegal holds**, **stalling** tactics, and **fleeing** the mat are infractions of the rules and will draw penalties.

Individual Match Points

Takedown	2 points
Escape	1 point
Reversal	2 points
Near Fall	2 or 3 points
Riding Time Advantage	1 point, maximum

If the competitors are tied at the end of the three regulation periods, a 2-minute sudden death **overtime** is held. Whoever scores first, wins. If the score remains tied, there is a 30-second **tiebreaker**, and whoever scores first, wins. If there is no scoring, the offensive wrestler is the winner.

Summary of Rules

Folkstyle

Time: Three periods
7 minutes (3-2-2)

Fall: Any part of both shoulders in contact with the mat for one second

Match Termination: 15-point advantage

Major Decision: 8-14 points after 3 periods

Decision: Fewer than 8 points after 3 periods

Overtime: If tied at end of regulation, a 2-minute sudden death overtime. Wrestler who scores first wins.

Tiebreaker: If no winner after 2-minute sudden death period, a 30-second tiebreaker. Whoever scores first, wins. If neither scores, the offensive wrestler wins.

International

Time: Two 3-minute periods

Fall (Pin): Both shoulders held on mat

Technical Fall: 10-point margin

Decision: Wrestler scores more points in bout

Overtime: If neither scores at least 3 points in regulation, a 3-minute overtime period will take place. If neither reaches 3 points, the officials decide the winner.

Tie Scores: 3-minute sudden death overtime. If tie not broken, officials decide the winner.

As in high school wrestling, there is a specific end-of-bout procedure to follow, in which the wrestlers wait for the decision from the scorer's table, the referee announces the decision, and the wrestlers shake hands. If the procedures are not observed by the contestants, an unsportsmanlike-conduct penalty is assessed. Behavior such as spitting, baiting your opponent, or throwing your headgear falls into this category and will result in a penalty being called against you and/or your team.

For more information on intercollegiate athletics, contact the NCAA at the address below:

National Collegiate Athletic Association (NCAA)
700 W. Washington Street Box 6222
Indianapolis, IA 46206-6222
Tel: (317) 917-6222 Fax: 317/917-6888
www.ncaa.org

Wrestling for Fun

If you belong to a wrestling club, there will be many opportunities for you to meet and compete with wrestlers from other clubs. These matches are usually low-key and provide experience and fun without the pressures of formal competitions.

Friendship Meets take place when two or four clubs get together for a day-long event of three wrestling matches to practice techniques. These meets give you a chance to show your favorite hold(s). At friendship meets, there are no winners or losers, no awards are given, and there are no tournament costs.

Ribbon Tournaments are also low-key, with no weight classes, medals, or champions; no one is eliminated by a loss. Wrestlers are grouped as nearly as possible by size, experience, and ability, and everyone who participates receives a certificate. Winners get a certificate with a blue ribbon on it; losers get a red ribbon. The second round matches winners versus winners and losers versus losers of the first round. By the end of the day, nearly all participants have blue and red ribbons on their certificates, but the important thing is to have fun and make new friends.

A **Technique Competition** shows how well you can execute different moves. Judging is based on your ability to execute particular maneuvers. You'll need a partner for support while executing a move and will probably take on this supporting role yourself. There will be judges—at least three—sitting around the edge of the mat and awarding scores of 1-10 points to each wrestler. Each move is scored, and the wrestler with the highest point total for a certain move is champion of that move and receives a certificate or ribbon for his victory.

Tournaments, while real competitions, are still meant to be fun and are a chance to meet other young wrestlers from different areas. Often, medals, ribbons, or trophies are given in each weight class.

There are many opportunities for wrestlers of all ages, weights, and skill levels to improve their skills and techniques to the point where they are able to compete on the national and international levels. A sport that usually begins as fun and "roughhousing" as a kid can become a worthwhile challenge governed by the mental and physical self-discipline that can bring the satisfaction of long-lasting accomplishments. Information on wrestling clubs in your area can be obtained from:

USA Wrestling
6155 Lehman Drive
Colorado Springs, CO 80918
Tel: (719) 598-8181 Fax: (719) 598-9440
www.usawrestling.com

7

Health and Physical Fitness

You can't succeed in any sport without getting into and maintaining good health and physical fitness. A major fringe benefit of wrestling is that the fitness you develop while learning and training for that sport will carry over to any other sports or recreational activities you enjoy—for example, soccer, biking, gymnastics, or swimming.

Nutrition

Good eating habits go hand-in-hand with fitness training. An athlete can be in good health without being physically fit, but he can't become physically fit without following a well-balanced diet that contains protein, fats, and carbohydrates in the proper amounts.

Carbohydrates are sugars and starches and come in two forms—simple and complex. The simple form, found in processed foods like candy, soft drinks, or sweet desserts, is the one to avoid. These provide only "empty" calories that may taste good momentarily, but do nothing for overall health. This is low-quality nutrition. It's not necessary to eliminate such foods entirely from your diet, but be selective. (Your dentist will be happy, too.)

Sugar, in its natural form, is abundant in fresh fruit, and a better way to satisfy a sweet-tooth is by eating a piece of fruit, rather than a candy bar.

Snacking in front of the television seems to be another American dietary habit, but for the athlete who is serious about wrestling and getting fit, there is no place for high-fat, high-salt, high-calorie "junk food" in his diet. Try munching on an apple, tangerine, or carrot or celery sticks while you watch your favorite show or when you need a snack during the day.

The U.S. Department of Agriculture (USDA) and the Department of Health and Human Services (DHHS) reissued "Dietary Guidelines for Americans" in May 2000. These revised guidelines emphasized the importance of carbohydrates and the lesser role of protein and fats in a healthful nutrition program.

Complex carbohydrates are an athlete's best nutritional friend because they are a primary source of fuel. You'll find them in bread, vegetables of all colors (especially peas and beans), fruit, nuts, pasta, and whole grains (wheat, rice, corn, and oats). They should make up about 60 percent of your well-balanced, nutritious meals throughout the day, starting with the first one.

Protein is found in many foods—nuts, dairy products, lean meats, poultry, and low-fat fish. You don't need a 16-ounce steak every day to "build muscle." In fact, that's probably too much protein for your body to absorb efficiently; the rest just goes to waste. Try to keep your protein consumption to about 20 percent of what you eat each day, and you'll consume enough to build muscle, maintain it, and repair it when necessary.

Your body does need some fat, but not nearly as much as most Americans consume every day from a diet that is often overloaded with fat and salt. The fat you eat should come from margarine, vegetable oil, or nuts and should be no more than 20 percent of your daily intake of food. Fat has some benefits; it is an insulator in cold weather and an energy source. But a little goes a long way to keep an athlete healthy and fit.

A Guide to Daily Food Choices

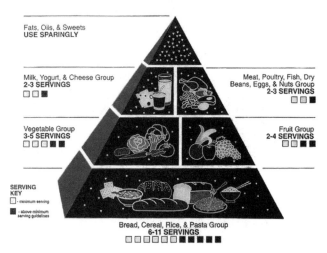

Source: U.S. Department of Agriculture and the
U.S. Department of Health and Human Services

Don't skip meals—especially breakfast. Breakfast is like putting gas in your car—you need it to get started—and that meal should be a good solid one-third of your daily calorie intake. Not hungry for breakfast in the morning? Try this once: Eat a light dinner the night before. You'll have an appetite in the morning, and that should help get you on a regular meal schedule. It maybe a cliché, but eating breakfast will make you feel better all day. Also, there is no nutritional law that requires a "traditional" breakfast. There is nothing wrong with eating a baked potato, having a hearty soup, or eating lean meat, fish, or poultry at your first meal of the day. The important point to learn is to eat well-balanced, nutritious meals throughout the day, starting with your first one.

A word on liquids: Avoid cola drinks, coffee, and tea. They are loaded with caffeine and act as diuretics to take water from your body. The one liquid you should not avoid is water, which is 60 percent of your body's weight and is needed to lubricate your joints and maintain body temperature. Water is also the transportation system for the nutrients you need to stay healthy, so don't neglect this crucial liquid. One to two quarts per day will keep your body well-lubricated and prevent dehydration.

The new dietary guidelines from the USDA and DHHS suggest that Americans ". . . limit the intake of beverages and foods that are high in added sugars." For example, a Food and Drug Administration (FDA) study, published early in 2000, reported that soda consumption per person in the United States had reached 41 gallons in 1997. This is nearly double the 1970 consumption rate of 22 gallons. A 12-ounce can of soda contains nine teaspoons of sugar, an amount that you could visualize by measuring this amount into a cup or glass. The size of soda containers has kept pace with consumption, from the standard 6.5-ounce bottle of the 1950s to today's 12-, 20-, and 64-ounce containers. As soda consumption has gone up, milk, juice, and water consumption has gone down. High-calorie soft drinks don't contain the vitamins and minerals needed for good health, so limiting your consumption is probably a good idea.

A recent study at Harvard University of adolescent girls (whose bones are maturing) indicates that many are drinking more sodas, not eating calcium-rich foods, and not getting enough weight-bearing exercise, such as running or tennis. Long range, these dietary deficits can lead to thin, brittle bones that fracture easily.

The problem is of such concern that the DHHS, the Centers for Disease Control (CDC), and the National Osteoporosis Foundation are cooperating in an information campaign aimed at 9- to 12-year-old girls. The campaign will stress the importance of calcium in the diet, which foods are good sources of calcium, and the importance of combining weight-bearing exercise with calcium intake.

The guidelines also made statements about exercise and sodium (salt) in the diet. For the first time, Americans are urged to include "moderate daily exercise" of at least 30 minutes per day in their lifestyles and to ". . . choose and prepare foods with less salt." This means avoiding soy sauce, ketchup, mustard, pickles, and olives.

For youngsters, weight should not be controlled, but in older athletes it can be managed in a healthy way. Coaches today place far more emphasis on weight management through a proper nutritional program. In fact, at the high school level, wrestling coaches are required to have a weight management program in place. This ensures that the wrestler will not lose strength or muscle but will perform at the weight class that is right for his body type. Your coaches will discuss body type and weight with you and decide in which age-weight category you belong. Try to maintain the weight level they recommend, and gain or lose weight according to their instructions. Follow their advice, and that of your parents, family doctor, or health care professional, about the diet and fitness training program that are best for you.

Bulimia and *anorexia nervosa* are two psychological and physical illnesses with their own forms of addictive behavior. Both young women and men have adopted these two damaging approaches to weight control. *Bulimics* try to diet, but then go on eating binges and follow up by purging themselves with laxatives, vomiting, or using diuretics. What begins as an attempt to control weight can become an ustoppable and extremely self-destructive habit requiring professional care.

Anorexics diet beyond just weight loss, and go to the extreme measure of starvation. If a person does not eat, the body takes energy from muscle tissue, including the heart. Such muscle damage can lead to heart failure and death. Like bulimics, anorexics need help from a professional. Karen Carpenter, a pop singer of the 1970s who had won three Grammys, and whose records had sold 30 million copies, died in 1983 of cardiac arrest brought on by years of being anorexic. She was only 32.

Therapists agree that these two eating disorders stem from low self-esteem, a poor body image, and a desire to be perfect. The perfection, however, is often based on an unrealistic standard that is also unattainable, *i.e.*, trying to have a tall and thin body like the male and female models often seen in magazine and television advertisements.

If you suspect you have an eating disorder, help is available from these groups:

National Association of Anorexia Nervosa and Associated Disorders (ANAD)
P.O. Box 7
Highland Park, IL 60035
(708) 831–3438
American Anorexia/Bulimia Association, Inc. (AABA)
418 East 76th St.
New York, NY 10021
(212) 734–1114
Overeaters Anonymous (OA)
4025 Spencer St., Suite 203
Torrance, CA 90504
(213) 542–8363

Finally, there are no "miracle foods" or "miracle diets" or "miracle pills" that will keep you in perfect health and physically fit. A well-balanced diet, paired with regular exercise, will help you stay in shape for life.

Rapid Weight Reduction Rule

USAW has adopted the following rule regarding rapid weight reduction. It is reprinted with the consent of USAW.

> *Whereas rapid weight reduction "cutting weight" through caloric restriction, dehydration, and excessive exercise in heated environments exposes wrestlers to decreased performance, heat-related trauma, and hazard to health and life, USA Wrestling (USAW) has adopted the following rules:*

> *With regard to the practice of dehydration, the use of hot rooms, hot showers, hot boxes, saunas, steam rooms, heating devices, diuretics, emetics, laxatives, excessive food and fluid restriction and self-induced vomiting is prohibited by USA Wrestling.*

> *Regardless of purpose, the use of vapor-impermeable suits (e.g., rubber or rubberized nylon) is prohibited.*

> *Violation of these rules of USAW sanctioned events shall cause the individual(s) in question to be suspended from the competition for which use of the prohibited methods were intended.*

> *Enforcement for this rule shall be the responsibility of the tournament committee which is to be established prior to the competition. The decision of the tournament committee shall be final.*

> *A second event violation will result in the suspension of the individual(s) from any USAW sanctioned event for one calendar year from time of suspension. All second*

violation cases shall be heard by the appropriate age group executive committee. USAW's By-laws shall be considered in all applicable cases.

Any individual assisting an athlete in prohibited weight reduction practices shall be held to the same rules and penalties as athletes.

USAW discourages rapid weight reduction methods under any circumstances. However, events excluded from these rules are Senior-level FILA calendar events and Senior-level FILA "world level championships" and those Senior-level competitions which are qualifying events for Senior-level FILA "world level championships."

Guidelines for applying the rule are:

- *This rule shall be in effect for all USAW sanctioned events (except those excluded above).*

- *The tournament committee of each event must put its decision in writing to both the offending party and the USA Wrestling National Office.*

- *The rule will be posted/distributed at the competition venue(s), weigh-in site(s), practice venue(s), host hotel(s), training site(s), and official housing facilities. In addition announcements will be made on the public address system throughout the weigh-ins, if possible, and during the competition.*

Precautions

Approximately 40-50 million Americans smoke, and studies have shown that most of them began in their early teens. The use of cigarettes by teenagers is growing, and several steps are being proposed to limit sales to those younger than 18. The number of cigarettes smoked and the percentage of smokers have declined steadily over the last 15 years, but "social smoking"—those who smoke occasionally—is up. Social smokers often have a sense that cigarettes are not harmful to health or an addiction, even though they are.

Based on recent statistical evidence from the Tobacco Intervention Network, young males seem most addicted to smokeless tobacco, wanting to imitate professional athletes or succumbing to peer pressure.

Smokeless tobacco causes dental cavities—it is one-third sugar. The irritation caused by holding a wad of tobacco in the mouth causes receding gums, gum disease, bone loss, and the inevitable tooth loss.

All drugs have side effects, and smokeless tobacco is no different. It increases blood pressure and heart rate, and seems to increase the likelihood of kidney disease. Smokeless tobacco does not improve an athlete's reaction time. Both the National Institute of Drug Abuse and the American Psychological Association agree that smokeless tobacco can produce dependency and result in addiction, with negative consequences for health and fitness.

The use of any tobacco product by officials is not strictly prohibited but is certainly not recommended. Coaches, wrestlers, and team personnel at the high school level, however, are considered guilty of unsportsmanlike conduct if they use tobacco products.

In 1994, a national study found that smoking marijuana had significantly increased between 1992 and 1994 among teens. The Partnership for a Drug-Free America believes that there is an epidemic, yet many youngsters think smoking marijuana is not dangerous and is a "safe" alternative to alcohol or tobacco. Because there was less marijuana smoking in the 1980s, many young people have not seen "pothead burnout" among adults or their peers and are ignorant of the consequences.

The ramifications of smoking marijuana have not been publicized, but 30 years of research have pinpointed the effects of this drug. According to Monika Guttman, who writes extensively about drug use, "marijuana reduces coordination; slows reflexes, interferes with the ability to measure distance, speed, and time; and disrupts concentration and short-term memory." (Everything on that list would be detrimental to any athlete, especially wrestlers.) Marijuana has six times as many carcinogens (cancer-causing agents) as tobacco, and today's marijuana is much more potent, creates dependency faster, and often becomes an "entrance" drug—one that can lead to dependence on "hard" drugs like cocaine.

Currently, nearly 12.5 million Americans use illegal drugs, and teenagers are the fastest growing portion of first-time, illegal drug users. The message Americans need to hear is that drugs are illegal, addictive, dangerous, unhealthy, and wrong. Teens know that drugs are the most important problem they face—above violence, sex issues, and getting into college. Drug-prevention materials for young people and adults are available by calling the U.S. Department of Health and Human Services at this toll-free number:

1-800-729-6686

Drugs of some type have been used by many athletes for many years. We don't expect this from Olympic competitors, but we know this is true. One reason given for taking drugs is to win medals. Perhaps that is why such drugs have been misnamed "performance enhancing," although in reality they are not. Steroids, amphetamines, hormones, human growth hormone (hGH), and erythropoietin (EPO) are a few drugs specifically banned by the IOC.

Steroids (anabolic-androgenic steroids, or AAS) are another drug danger, with terrible consequences for the user. Steroid use by males can result in breast development, hair loss, and acne, plus yellow skin and eyes. Among females, breasts shrink, hair grows on the face and body, and menstrual cycles can become irregular. For both males and females, the result of steroid use can be permanent stunting of body growth.

The food additive androstenedione, or "andro," has been identified as a steroid and is now illegal without medical reasons. On their own initiative, the IOC, the National Football League (NFL), the NCAA, and other sports organizations have already banned its use by athletes.

The psychological effects of steroid use are just as devastating, according to the American Sports Education Institute, which has noted the following: "Wide mood swings ranging from periods of violent, even homicidal, episodes known as 'roid rages' to depression, paranoid jealousy, extreme irritability, delusions, and impaired judgment."

The American Medical Association, the IOC, the NCAA, and the NFL have deplored the use of steroids for muscle building or improving athletic performance.

The negative impacts on an athlete's health of using EPO, for example, can range from sterility to the risk of heart attack, liver and kidney disease, and some cancers. These are permanent, not temporary, health problems. EPO has caused deaths in athletes, as have amphetamines, and no one knows yet the long-term effects on a normal-sized person of using human growth hormone.

A partial list of the consequences of taking any of these drugs follows:

- Creatine: The side effects are dizziness, diarrhea, and cramps.
- EPO: Forces the heart to work harder. Can cause heart attacks and strokes and sudden death.
- Anabolic steroids: Higher cholesterol, "roid rages," perhaps liver disease and cancer, heart disease, brain

tumors. Among women, hair on the face, lost hair from the head, acne, breast shrinkage, and cessation of menstrual periods.

- Cyproterone acetate: Stops sexual development in women.

- hGH: The side effects are unusual bone growth (acromegaly). The forehead, cheeks, jaw, hands, and feet grow grotesquely.

- Amphetamines: Temporary boosters that increase heart rate, blood pressure, and respiration. They do not boost performance levels; in fact, they actually decrease them.

Vision and Dental Care

If you wear corrective lenses and want to wrestle, talk to your eye doctor and ask him if contact lenses would be suitable for you. Today's contacts come in hard and soft materials, are lightweight, and some can be worn for hours at a time. In fact, there are disposable contact lenses that can be worn 24 hours a day, don't need special cleaning, and can be disposed of after seven days. The latter are fairly expensive, however, and may not be suitable for the young, growing athlete. Always check with your doctor and get his recommendations for your unique needs. If you wear the traditional contacts, be sure to have your cleaning and wetting solutions with you at practices and competitions, and let your coach know you wear contacts.

Wearing a mouth guard can prevent injury to your teeth, lips, cheeks, and gums, so use it at practices and competitions. Concussions or other head and neck injuries can be minimized by wearing a properly fitted mouth guard made by your dentist. It is not bulky, will not restrict your breathing, fits snugly, and covers your front teeth so well that you'll hardly know you're wearing it.

No matter what sport you play, custom mouth guards can help prevent oral injuries. They are especially important for young children just starting out in sports. In fact, if you get used to wearing one early, it will be easier to continue wearing one at the high school or collegiate levels, where competition is far more aggressive.

Physical Fitness and Conditioning

It is never too soon or too late to begin exercising and getting your body into good working order. If you are overweight, get winded easily, or are otherwise out of shape, you may have difficulty participating in wrestling. Consult your physician, however, before beginning any fitness program, and work only under the supervision of a qualified, knowledgeable coach or trainer.

The Four Parts of Fitness

Physical fitness has four parts: muscle strength, muscle endurance, cardiovascular (heart, lungs, and blood vessels) endurance, and flexibility. Each part depends on the others to maintain physical fitness. Push-ups, for example, build strong muscles through muscle repetition. Muscle endurance aims to work muscles over a period of time without tiring them. Sit-ups are great for this. Muscles need oxygen to function at peak levels, and this is why the heart, lungs, and blood vessels are so important to physical fitness. They sustain working muscles over long periods of time during practice sessions and wrestling matches.

Muscle Strength

Muscle strength can prevent aches and pains, keep the body aligned properly, and prevent injuries. Building this muscle strength requires fast and long exercise. The muscle gets "tired," but this is what builds strength. Muscles should feel a little uncomfortable, but not painful. The goal is all-over muscle strength, since too much strength in one group of muscles can lead to an injury in another group. Strong muscles with low flexibility can lead to muscle pulls, while flexibility with low muscle strength can lead to dislocations.

Whether you use hand-held dumbbells or sophisticated exercise machines, strength-training techniques work the same way: they pit your muscles against resistance. (An athlete using equipment at a gym needs guidance from a fitness trainer.) Strength grows as resistance is increased, a concept called "progressive overload." Repeated stress thickens the fibers that make up muscles by increasing protein buildup. The thicker the muscle fibers, the stronger the muscles. A strength-training session includes exercises for all the major muscle groups. This type of training is done in sets of 8-12 repetitions, using a weight just heavy enough so that only 12 repetitions can be produced.

Some suggested muscle-strength exercises are abdominal curls for a strong abdomen and lower back, and squats for strong shoulders, hips, lower buttocks, thighs, calves, and ankles. Lifting two 3-pound weights, which can be books, quart bottles filled with water, or standard weights purchased at a sporting goods store, is good for building strength in arm muscles. (There are ankle, body, and wrist weights also.) Take a day off in-between workouts to give muscles recovery and muscle-building time.

Muscle Endurance

Muscle-endurance exercises build stamina to help the body perform at its best. This training repeats the same exercise many times, using a relatively light weight. Vigorous exercises, such as jogging, bicycling, and swimming, are excellent for achieving muscle endurance. They also increase heart and lung efficiency and improve an athlete's overall personal appearance. Muscle-endurance training should only be done three times a week because muscle fibers tear slightly during exercise and need rest to rebuild themselves.

Cardiovascular Endurance

Cardiovascular endurance is achieved through exercises performed for at least 20 minutes. Walking, jogging, running, bicycling, swimming, dancing, and skipping rope are activities that raise the heart rate, take oxygen into the body, and move it to the muscles, which then provide the energy for the exercise that is being done.

Weather and unhealthful air sometimes interfere with outdoor endurance exercises, so gyms have become more and more popular with athletes. Stationary bicycles are widely available and can be "ridden" to fit a personal schedule that is not dependent on the weather. Other indoor endurance exercises include jogging in place, doing jumping jacks, and doing side hops. When exercising on a rug, wear gym socks; on a hard floor, shoes that cushion the feet are best.

Flexibility

There are numerous flexibility exercises—bends, stretches, swings, twists, lifts, and raisers—which stretch out muscles that have "tightened" from vigorous exercise. Muscle-pull injuries are common when flexibility is poor, even though muscle strength might be high. On the other hand, when flexibility is high but muscle strength low, dislocations can occur.

Stretching and Warming Up

Regardless of your age, it's important that your body be flexible and relaxed. One of the best ways to maintain flexibility and to relax muscles is to stretch every day. Do not pull the body into exaggerated or painful positions. That is not stretching; that is torture. Such extremes are not helpful and may even cause an injury. Follow a few simple guidelines for effective stretching. Before you practice any of the seven basic wrestling skills, you need to do a short series of stretching and warm-up exercises. The point of stretching is to get the blood flowing and to "loosen" the muscles and tendons, which will help your flexibility—a major requirement in wrestling—and can reduce your chances of a pulled muscle or injury. Stretching exercises should start from the top, at the neck, and work down to the legs, with arm, shoulder, and lower back exercises in between. Do each slowly and never stretch to a point that is painful. Motions should be fluid, and the exercises done at a slow to medium pace, preferably in a warm environment. Remember to drink plenty of fluids, especially in warm weather. The body's lymph nodes need fluid to carry away impurities; without adequate fluids, the circulatory system cannot function effectively.

- Start with both feet on the ground, weight balanced over the balls of the feet. Let arms hang loosely at sides. Wiggle fingers; then gently shake wrists. Next, shake arms. Rest.

- Raise arms and "reach for the sky." Roll up on the toes and stretch, reaching as high as possible with one hand. Hold this position for ten seconds, then reach with the other hand and hold. Repeat this exercise five times.

- Rest hands on hips and, keeping the back straight and head forward, stretch to the left. Hold. Now arch the right arm over the head so that the fingers point to the left and down. Hold. (There should be a gentle stretch along the right side of the body.) Do the same exercise with the left arm, fingers pointing to the right and down. Hold. Repeat this exercise five times.

- Rest hands on hips and bend forward from the waist. Do not bounce. Stretch gently and hold. Tilt the chin down toward the chest, remove hands from hips, and let arms hang loosely. Wiggle fingers and shake arms. (There should be a gentle stretch along the backs of legs, up through the back and neck.) Return, slowly and smoothly without jerking, to a standing position and rest.

To stretch legs, move to an area where there is something sturdy to hang onto and ample room to swing the legs freely.

- Stand with feet about 8-9 inches apart. Upper torso should be balanced over the hips, head up (but not tilted back), and the eyes looking forward. Body should be straight but not stiff. If right-handed, shift the weight to the left leg and begin the exercise with the right leg. If left-handed, reverse the order. Hold onto a chair or other support with the left hand and gently swing the right leg forward and backward 15 times. Turn around. Do the exercise 15 times swinging the opposite leg. Rest.

- Hold onto a support structure and balance the weight over the left leg. Stick the right leg out in front, toes up toward the sky, heel no more than 6 inches off the ground. Now, with the back straight but not stiff, push the right heel forward—not down toward the ground, but forward. The calf muscle should stretch. Do not bounce. Hold for a count of 10 seconds, return heel and toes to starting position, and lower the right leg to the ground. Balance the weight equally over both feet, and rest. Turn around and repeat the exercise with the opposite leg.

After completing the stretching exercises, keep your body warm.

Just as the neophyte wrestler learns the seven basic skills, so too does he work on a conditioning program to build muscle strength and endurance, which can reduce the chance of an injury. Before you practice any of those seven basic skills, you need to do a short series of warm-up exercises. These will get your muscles warm and loose and make your heart beat faster, so you'll be ready for the falls and physical contact of wrestling practice.

A few good warm-ups at this stage are jogging, doing somersaults (both forward and backward), jumping, hopping, and with a partner, doing a wheelbarrow and carrying your partner "piggyback."

With a partner, or partners, you can do warm-up exercises that combine some wrestling moves. Naturally, you will do these exercises under the supervision of your coach:

> The fireman's carry
> A quarter-nelson
> Hand control
> Knee to chest
> Two-man pull-ups
> Four-man push-ups

Squats are the leg strength-building exercises you've probably done already with a partner when you've been practicing how to lift properly. They're repeated here as a reminder.

The **back arch** and **back bridge hip heist** are two exercises for the advanced wrestler and should only be attempted when your coach says you're ready.

Following a program of sensible eating habits, along with physical fitness and conditioning, can help to prevent setbacks in your wrestling program. The healthy, fit athlete is the one who will perform at his best and will truly enjoy the sport.

Conditioning Programs
Many wrestlers play other sports to stay in shape and keep their stamina level high in the off-season. Year-round conditioning is advocated by some coaches who prepare their athletes by dividing the year into phases or periods, with different goals and objectives for each period. Coaches at the highest levels of competition expect several hours per day of fitness training because they know that athletes who stay fit are less likely to sustain injuries and will recover faster when they are injured.

Reconditioning

As important as conditioning programs are, a program of reconditioning is equally important after an athlete has suffered an injury. Athletes want to compete, but the decision to return to competition should be made by the player's parents, family physician, and coach, all working together.

A sprained ankle, for example, might be rehabilitated with easy jogging at first and then building up to running. Ice can be used to reduce any swelling that might occur, and/or an elastic bandage might be worn.

Everyone involved should be patient and not allow the athlete to return to play until the injury is no longer a problem. Semi-recovered wrestlers can reinjure themselves and set back their recovery time.

Note: This book is in no way intended to be a substitute for the medical advice of a personal physician. We advise and encourage the reader to consult with his/her physician before beginning this or any other weight-management, exercise, or fitness program. The authors and the publisher disclaim any liability or loss, personal or otherwise, resulting from the suggestions in this book.

8

Safety and First Aid

Wrestling is one of the safer sports for young athletes, but learning a few common safety rules can prevent serious injury. Since all athletes get bumps and bruises, and occasionally more serious injuries, here are a few precautions to take whenever you practice or compete:

Safety First

- Always wear your headgear to practices and competitions. It's designed to protect you from injury and is required for all younger athletes. If your dentist has recommended a mouth guard, be sure to have it in your mouth during practices and competitions.

- Wear the right clothes for practice sessions. Don't wear "cutoff" pants with zippers or rivets or a belt with a metal buckle. They can scratch or gouge. Your gym shorts with a drawstring or elastic waist are best.

- Leave any jewelry in your locker or duffel bag. That includes watches, rings, earrings, etc. This rule applies to both boys and girls.

- Your coaches, or a designated helper, should make certain that there is extra room around the practice mats so you won't bump into furniture, walls, or other wrestlers. Occasionally, you might have to practice on mats that are not exactly the same as the ones used in tournaments. These should be put together with tape so they don't slip and slide during a practice or bout. This can prevent unnecessary injuries, even minor ones, and a vinyl mat cover can be useful as well in preventing some injuries.

- Pay attention to your teammates and point out anything hazardous they might be doing. It's easy to get hurt just "fooling around," so don't do this yourself, and discourage your teammates from any activity that might cause an injury.

- Go through a warm-up session and do your stretching exercises before the actual practice or competition begins. This will prevent muscle strains and other aches and pains. If you're competing in a wrestling match that is interrupted for some reason, put on a robe or some kind of covering to keep warm. Cold muscles are more susceptible to injury.

- If you're not feeling well, skip a practice or two. You'll make a quicker recovery and be in better shape than if you practiced or competed while "under the weather."

- Drink plenty of water. Dehydration can happen quickly, so don't wait until you're thirsty to get a drink. Your coaches can recommend a sports drink, if they think such products are useful, but water tastes just as good and is usually free, with no cans or bottles to dispose of.

The First Aid Kit
Coaches know that eventually someone will probably sustain

an injury of some kind. So, it's wise to know what to do to handle those inevitable bumps, bruises, scrapes, or more serious injuries. Having a well-stocked first aid kit handy is recommended. The basics in it should include the following:

• Adhesive tape in different sizes

• Adhesive bandages in different shapes and sizes

• Ammonia caps for dizziness

• Antiseptic solution for minor scrapes

• Antiseptic soap for washing a wounded area

• Aspirin, or its equivalent, for simple headaches. (For youth teams, no medication should be given without written, parental permission, signed and dated, authorizing the disbursement of aspirin, or any other medicine.)

• Blanket to cover an injured player, since warmth reduces the chance of shock

• Cold packs

• Elastic wraps of various sizes

• Eyewash solution

• Gauze pads

• Hank's solution (trade name, Save-A-Tooth®) for a knocked-out tooth

• Plastic bottle filled with fresh water

• Sterile cotton sheets that can be cut to fit

• Scissors and perhaps an eyedropper and tweezers

• Tissues and premoistened towelettes

• Disposable towels

• A spray bottle or aerosol can containing chlorine bleach

and water (a commercial disinfectant for cleaning blood from the mat may be used instead)

- Antiseptic to clean blood from the wrestler

- Protective gloves

- Saliva boxes lined with disposable plastic bags

Remember that Occupational Safety and Health Administration (OSHA) regulations must be followed when disposing of any items that have blood contamination.

It is a good idea to have a list of emergency telephone numbers taped inside the first aid kit, but in a real emergency, you can dial 911. Be sure you know where there's a telephone and have some spare change in the first aid kit. At large tournaments, it is wise to have a physician, nurse, or other trained health care professional on hand to take care of serious injuries should they occur. Never assume that precautions have been taken. Check in advance to be sure; be prepared.

Coaches may find these guidelines helpful:

- **Always remain calm.** Don't panic or appear flustered. Others around you will take their behavior cues from you.

- **Don't try to be a doctor.** When in doubt about the severity of any injury, send the player to his doctor, or let the doctor, nurse, or health care professional on duty at the wrestling match make the decision.

- **Never move a player who may have a serious injury.** Don't try to make the wrestler more comfortable by moving him off the mat or into the locker room. This can make a serious injury worse. Be safe, not sorry, and call in the designated professionals if you have doubts about any injury. Under no circumstances should an unconscious wrestler be moved! Stay with him until the professionals arrive.

Scrapes and Mat Burns

Wash scrapes and mat burns with an antiseptic cleaning solution and cover with sterile gauze. This is usually all that is needed to promote quick healing of these fairly common injuries.

Muscle Pulls, Sprains, and Bruises

Rest, ice, compression, and elevation (RICE) are the steps needed to handle these injuries and about all you should do in the way of treatment. RICE reduces the swelling of most injuries and speeds up recovery.

Have the wrestler stop and rest, apply ice, compress with an elastic bandage, and elevate the injured arm, leg, knee, or ankle. Ice reduces swelling and pain and should be left on the injured area until it feels uncomfortable. Remove the ice pack and rest for 15 minutes, then reapply. These are the immediate steps to take until the doctor arrives. Over the next few days, the injury should be treated with two to three 20-minute sessions per day at two and one-half hour intervals. This should provide noticeable improvement. Don't overdo the icing; 20 minues is long enough. In most cases, after two or three days, or when the swelling has stopped, heat can be applied in the form of warm-water soaks. Fifteen minutes of warm soaking, along with a gradual return to motion, will speed the healing process right along.

Another approach to use after two or three days, and if your doctor agrees, is to begin motion, strength, and alternative (MSA) exercise. The American Institute for Preventive Medicine recommends:

- **Motion:** Moving the injured area and reestablishing its range of motion.

- **Strength:** Working to increase the strength of the injured area once any inflammation subsides and your range of motion begins to return.

- **Alternative:** Regularly do an alternative exercise that does not stress the injury.

Seek the advice of a sports-medicine professional prior to starting your own treatment plan. Specially shaped pads are useful for knee and ankle injuries, and they can be used in combination with ice, compression, and elevation. For a simple bruise, apply an ice pack.

Head, Hand, and Foot Injuries

Blows to the upper part of the head, especially near the eyes, can cause bleeding under the skin and result in a black eye or eyes. An ice pack applied to the area will keep down the swelling until a doctor can look at the injury.

Normally, the eye can wash out most foreign particles with its ability to produce tears. If this doesn't work, use eye cleaning solution to wash out the irritant. A few simple guidelines to follow are:

- Don't rub your eye or use anything dirty, like a cloth or finger, to remove the irritant.

- With clean hands, pull the eyelid forward and down, as you look down at the floor.

- Flush with eyewash, or use a clean, sterile cloth to remove any particle you can see floating on the eye.

If the foreign object remains, the coach should tape a clean gauze pad over the eye and have the wrestler see a doctor.

Nosebleeds usually don't last very long. A wrestler with a nosebleed should sit quietly and apply a cold pack, while pinching the bleeding nostril at its base.

Communicable diseases such as boils, athlete's foot, ringworm, and cold sores are common afflictions among wrestlers. Mouth sores may be treated with an over-the-counter medication, but check with your coach or doctor first before using any of these. The best medicine, however, is prevention. You should avoid "skin-to-skin" contact with any wrestler who has any skin disorder.

A knocked-out tooth can be successfully replanted if it is stored and transported properly. The tooth should be placed in a transport container containing a solution, such as Hank's or Viaspan®, which is available over-the-counter at a drugstore. The coach and all medical personnel at a wrestling event should be alert to the importance of how to care for a knocked-out tooth. With immediate and proper attention to storage and transport, an injured wrestler may be able to have a knocked-out tooth replanted successfully.

Jammed and/or broken fingers can be hard to distinguish, so use a cold pack to control swelling and pain. If there is no improvement within an hour, send the wrestler for an X-ray.

Small cuts need pressure to slow down bleeding. Then wash with an antiseptic solution, cover with sterile gauze taped in place, and apply pressure. Of course, any deep or large cut might need stitches, so the wrestler should see a doctor as soon as possible.

Do not move a seriously injured wrestler. Instead, get prompt medical attention or call for emergency aid. If you will have to wait for assistance, cover the injured wrestler with a lightweight blanket, since warmth will reduce the chance of shock. A wrestler who has a broken bone should be seen by a doctor. To safely move a person with an arm, wrist, hand, or leg injury, follow these steps:

- A finger with mild swelling can be gently taped to an adjacent finger.

- An elastic bandage may be gently wrapped around an injured wrist to give the wrist support. Do not wrap heavily, and do not pull the bandage tight.

If the wrestler has a possible broken leg or arm, the best approach is not to move the leg or arm in any manner. A cold pack can be used to lessen discomfort until medical personnel arrive, and the wrestler should be kept warm with a blanket or covering to avoid shock.

Fractures and broken bones are the same whether the bone is cracked, chipped, or broken. A fracture can be recognized by some or all of the following:

- A part of the body is bent or twisted from its normal shape

- A bone has pierced the skin

- Swelling is severe and more than the swelling associated with a typical sprain or bruise

- Hand or foot becomes extremely cold, which may indicate pinching of a major blood vessel

Youngsters heal faster than adults, so it's important to get them prompt medical attention when a fracture occurs.

Blisters are fairly common problems for wrestlers. Well-fitting shoes and socks can go a long way toward preventing this annoying, painful injury. Any blisters that do occur should be kept clean and covered with a bandage, especially if the blister breaks. Over-the-counter medications to treat blisters are available, but follow your coach's or doctor's suggestions on these.

Breathing and Heat Problems

Getting the wind "knocked out of you" is going to happen. Not much can be done to prevent this, and not much can be done to treat this. Your breathing will return to normal faster if you can relax and take easy breaths.

Heat stroke and heat exhaustion do occur, but they can be minimized or avoided if wrestlers take plenty of water breaks. Coaches should monitor their wrestlers during practices and competitions to be sure the youngsters aren't getting dehydrated. If heat stroke or exhaustion do occur, have the wrestler lie down where it's cool and call an ambulance.

By following the guidelines in this chapter, the extent and severity of injuries can be reduced and treatment minimized, so the player can return to the mat confidently. Knowing what to do is beneficial to players, coaches, and parents in and out of the sport.

9

Guidelines

For everyone involved to get maximum enjoyment from a wrestling event, good sportsmanship must extend beyond the field of play—in wrestling's case, the mat—and include parents and spectators, as well as players and coaches.

Hints for Parents and Spectators

Wrestling is meant to be fun for everyone involved, so parents need to be supportive, be enthused about the sport, and keep it all in perspective by focusing on achievements rather than miscues. Those attitudes will build the confidence a youngster needs to succeed, not just in wrestling but in other activities as well. Parents, you are the earliest role models your children learn from and imitate, and they will carry over into sports the attitudes they have learned from you.

Parents want their kids to excel, to come out on top, and to be winners. Because wrestling is an individual one–on–one sport, there is always a winner and a loser. Parents must accept the fact that their child is going to lose sometimes, so they need to be prepared to handle defeat in an adult manner by praising the effort involved and avoiding a litany of "What you should have done was..." Most youngsters are pretty well aware of their skills, and they don't need to be told or made to feel somehow deficient when they lose. Likewise, parents should recognize the achievement of the victor and never criticize the officials or coaches.

Remember, coaches and officials are usually volunteers and are probably parents who have children involved in the sport. They feel as intensely as you do—perhaps even more so, since they are more directly involved. But they have to be objective, treat all players with the same respect and regard, and follow the rules. You should, too.

Before attending a wrestling match as a spectator, learn a few basics about the sport, and your enjoyment will increase along with your understanding. Knowing some of the basic skills—stance, lifting, penetration—will help you follow the action on the mat. Wrestling is fast—most regulation bouts are three to five minutes—so plan to watch as many as possible to get a "feel" for the sport. Knowing how points are scored is also helpful because some matches will be decided on points

Thumbs Up

The team is ready for a match

scored, rather than a pin or a fall. Observing a few common courtesies—sitting in your seat, not blocking anyone's view, not shouting at the officials, not criticizing the form or technique of a player, not arguing with other spectators—will make you a welcome spectator at any match. Any spectator who behaves in a manner that is considered unsportsmanlike conduct will be asked to leave the match.

Teams and Wrestlers

A truism of all sports is that learning to be a member of a team is one of life's crucial skills. Working together toward a goal rewards everyone involved with a sense of accomplishment, achievement, and pride in the effort. Win or lose, everyone learns from the experience.

Mutual aid and dependability are needed from all members of a team, so be supportive of your teammates and let them know you can be depended upon to show up for practices and games. There are a few specific things you can do for yourself and your team:

• Support each wrestler. Offer encouragement, especially in defeat, and congratulations in victory.

• Use positive, not negative, reinforcement. Point out the good holds and techniques.

• Let your coach correct errors. That's his job.

• Don't be a show-off.

• Try your best, go to every practice, and show that you are trying. Don't dwell on "mistakes"— yours or anyone else's.

• Never be guilty of taunting—on or off the mat.

• Set a good example by staying healthy and physically fit.

• Remember, using tobacco products is considered unsportsmanlike conduct for players as well as coaches and team personnel.

As an individual wrestler, you need to keep the sport in perspective and fit it into your entire life, which means assigning priorities. You'll have to stay fit and healthy and get enough sleep each night. Since many schools require that a certain level of academic achievement be maintained in order to participate in sports, school attendance and schoolwork cannot be neglected in favor of concentrating on athletics. For you, wrestling can be a rewarding experience, if you remember the following:

- Compete because you want to. Don't let someone "pressure" you into wrestling.
- Obey the rules.
- Don't argue, whine, or gripe about calls or decisions.
- Keep your temper in hand and never retaliate.
- Prepare, do your best, and have fun.
- Finally, the Golden Rule does work. Treat everyone the way you want to be treated.

Being a dependable member of your team, learning from your coaches, following their guidelines, and playing fair with opponents can make your wrestling experience a lifelong guide to achieving other goals.

Wrestlers should behave in such a way that they are a credit to their schools, the sport, and themselves. The image of the sport depends on your behavior and appearance, not only at matches, but also while traveling, and at school or away. Your conduct can influence your teammates as well as whether or not you win or lose.

Coaches

Just as parents are the first "real life" role models for children, teachers and coaches come next. Coaches have immediate and quite visible responsibilities to their charges, so set the example you want them to follow. Be on time for practices, keep yourself fit and healthy, praise and criticize positively. Kids develop an intuitive alarm that goes off when someone breaks the rules. Be fair, and never use your position of authority to gain an unfair advantage for yourself or your wrestlers.

Thumbs Up

Spectators

The use of tobacco products by coaches draws an unsportsmanlike conduct penalty in scholastic wrestling, so it is important to know the rules and enforce them uniformly, not only with the wrestlers but also with other team personnel. Taunting others is expressly prohibited and can result in the coach, his wrestlers, the team, and other personnel being hit with an unsportsmanlike conduct penalty.

The ethical obligations of coaches are broad and deep and extend beyond practices and competitions to include other members of the academic and nonacademic wrestling communities. Building character, integrity, and respect and ensuring the physical well-being of your wrestlers are integral parts of your coaching duties and should be included in the total learning experience of young wrestlers.

10

Wrestling Wrap-up

The Benefits of Wrestling

Wrestling is an equal opportunity sport—it's for every kid—short or tall, chubby or skinny. Because of its age and weight category system, kids are never overmatched, which could be demoralizing or intimidating. This is a sport where everyone participates since there are no "benchwarmers" or "subs" or "designated hitters." Wrestling has a soft impact on the pocketbook, too, for no large investment in bats, balls, gloves, rackets, expensive lessons, or fancy gear is required. This is a sport where any individual can go all-out to win, not half-wrestle to avoid a loss.

Wrestling is a very "natural" activity that most youngsters seem to engage in at some time or another—on the floor in the family room, or outside in the yard. To channel this youthful energy, there is no better sport than wrestling. As a year-round activity, wrestling doesn't need a "season," which prevents the ups and downs of getting in shape. Wrestling teaches youngsters how to have a lifetime of good health and physical fitness, while the coordination, agility, and flexibility learned in wrestling can be used to advantage in other sports. Wrestlers learn teamwork, good sportsmanship, fair play, and the ability to get along with others in a competitive setting, while relying on the individual's skills. The sport involves entire families at many levels of competition, from elementary school through college and beyond. Besides, wrestlers make great role models. Many attend college and get their degrees in a range of academic disciplines.

Physically, wrestling builds muscles, flexibility, and strength. Proper coaching fosters good eating habits and warns of the health hazards of alcohol, tobacco, and drugs. Mentally, this one-on-one sport builds self-confidence and a "can-do" attitude. Wrestlers learn to set goals and how to achieve them. In this mental action/reaction sport, the wrestler must concentrate and think against one opponent. Wrestling teaches self-control and independence and instills the discipline needed to say no to temporary pleasures in favor of long-range rewards. Socially, a wrestler develops respect and admiration for others and their abilities. He learns to obey and play by the rules and to accept the decisions of adults. The wrestler gains valuable experience in teamwork, cooperation, and the need to subordinate his own wishes to that of an overall team effort.

Athletes with Special Needs – USABA

In 1976, the United States Association of Blind Athletes (USABA) was founded as a nonprofit member of the U.S. Olympic Committee to train blind and visually-impaired athletes for national and international competition. Its more than 3,000 members compete in nine sports: Alpine and Nordic skiing, goalball, judo, powerlifting, swimming, tandem cycling, track and field, and wrestling. USABA's major goal is to ensure that legally blind athletes get the same competitive opportunities as sighted athletes.

At the 1994 Winter Paralympic Games in Lillehammer,

Norway, athletes from USABA earned five medals—the highest count for blind athletes in the history of the Winter Games. Wrestling Nationals for USABA members were held in Indianapolis, IN, on March 29 and 30, 1996.

Additionally, USABA hosts more than 400 events every year for blind athletes, who have been able to train at the Olympic Training Centers in Colorado Springs, CO, and at Lake Placid, NY. The group is headquartered at the Colorado School for the Deaf and Blind in Colorado Springs, CO. Further information may be obtained by writing or calling:

USABA
33 N. Institute St.
Colorado Springs, CO 80903
(719) 630–0422

Volunteering

Being a volunteer requires some extra time and a desire to make a difference in the lives of young people. Wrestling is a golden opportunity for everyone in a family or the community at large to get involved and make this difference. Today more than ever, young people need to know adults care about them and their futures, since they are bombarded every day by enticements to use drugs, join gangs, or engage in other activities that promote a dangerous lifestyle.

There are many ways you can help your local wrestling club, as a coach or leader, official or fan. When a local club or school is sponsoring a tournament, you could volunteer to help in a number of ways:

• Help set up the area where competitions will take place.

• Staff the on-site registration table.

• Conduct the weigh-in or be a pairing chief.

• Be a timer, scorer, or runner.

- Be the announcer.

- Be the tournament coordinator.

Coaching

USAW has a four-level coach certification program—Copper, Bronze, Silver, and Gold—for its more than 10,000 active coaches. USAW also oversees the 2,000 officials who belong to the U.S. Wrestling Officials Association (USWOA). Educational programs for coaches cover a range of topics from psychology to strength training and diets for combating fatigue, along with explanations of the rules for coaches and wrestlers. Technique clinics are held to demonstrate offense and defense, so that wrestlers and coaches may improve their skills.

Organizations for Coaches and Officials

The National Wrestling Coaches Association (NWCA) includes members from both the collegiate and scholastic levels who meet regularly and network extensively.

The National Federation of Interscholastic Coaches Association (NFICA), and the National Federation of Interscholastic Officials Association (NFIOA) are the national groups for coaches and officials at the high school level. More information on these two groups can be obtained by contacting:

National Federation of State High School Associations
11724 Plaza Circle, Box 20626
Kansas City, MO 64195–0626
(816) 464–5400

National Wrestling Hall of Fame and Museum

A national museum for wrestling was the idea of Myron Roderick, the first executive director of USA Wrestling, and Dr. Melvin D. Jones, an insurance executive and avid wrestling fan. Funded by popular subscription, the museum was dedicated in 1976. Located near the campus of Oklahoma State University in Stillwater, OK, the National Wrestling Hall of Fame and Museum commemorates and celebrates the sport of wrestling in America.

The Hall has three major areas and themes. Great athletes, coaches, and contributors are spotlighted in the Honors Court. A Wall of Champions lists the names of 4,500 American wrestlers who have starred in national and international competitions. The library contains an expanding collection of materials on wrestling—books, films, and videos.

The Hall of Fame promotes wrestling nationwide and focuses on family participation so that parents are involved along with their children. The classic green marble sculpture *The Wrestlers,* which graces the lobby of the Museum and weighs more than three-quarters of a ton, is a copy of the original housed at the Uffizi Gallery in Florence, Italy.

For more information, contact the Hall of Fame at the address below:

National Wrestling Hall of Fame and Museum
405 W. Hall of Fame Ave.
Stillwater, OK 74075
Tel: (405) 377-5243 Fax: (405) 377-5244
www.wrestlinghalloffame.org

11

Glossary

Wrestling has its own vocabulary of terms and definitions unique to the sport, and a separate vocabulary for officials. (See the end of this chapter for a list of USA Wrestling terms and their FILA equivalents.)

General Terms and Definitions

Age A wrestler's age is the birthday he has during the calendar year. For example, if he becomes 15 in July 2000, he is considered 15 all year.

Amplitude A throw in which the opponent is lifted above the thrower's waist. Points differ for high and low amplitude throws.

Blind draw Drawing of lots. All positions are determined by chance. There is no seeding or separation.

Blue pool The wrestlers with even draw numbers.

Body lock When you lock your hands around your opponent's body to execute a throw.

Bout The competition between two wrestlers; a match.

Bridge	When a wrestler supports himself on his head, elbows, and feet to keep his shoulders from touching the mat.
Brutality	Unnecessary roughness. The motive is to injure your opponent. Penalty is disqualification from the tournament.
Cadet	The 15-16 age group for wrestlers.
Call to the mat	Two wrestlers are called to report to a specific mat for their competition.
Category	The age group in which a wrestler competes.
Caution	The penalty against a wrestler for an illegal hold, fleeing a hold, fleeing the mat, or refusing to take a starting position in *par terre*.
Center	Starting area in the center of the mat. Also, an instruction to the wrestlers to return to the center.
Central wrestling area	The middle of the mat, 7 meters across (in national and international competitions), where the action should take place.
Correct hold	A well-executed throw. Not a takedown, or putting the opponent in danger. A point may be awarded for "appreciation" of the throw.
Counter	A defensive action that stops or blocks the offensive wrestler's attack. Points can be awarded for a counter.
Decision	Victory on points. The margin can be from 1-9 points in international matches.

Default A bout ends in default when one wrestler is injured and can't compete.

Disqualification One or both wrestlers are eliminated from a bout.

Division Age group or category in which a wrestler competes. (*See* Category.)

DNWI Notation that a wrestler did not weigh in.

Drawing of lots The time when random selection of numbers by each wrestler at the weigh-in takes place.

Draw number Number drawn by lot to identify each wrestler.

Drug testing Ordered for any contestant at any time, at any national or international event or trials, at the request of FILA, the U.S. Olympic Committee or USA Wrestling.

Elimination Removal of a wrestler from the competition. A second defeat, an injury, forfeit, failure to weigh in, or misconduct can result in elimination.

Escape Wrestler gets out from under opponent, gets on his feet, and faces his opponent.

Exposure Occurs when the defensive wrestler's back is turned toward the mat. The head or an elbow are not touching the mat. Earns one point.

Face mask A protective cushion worn due to an injury. Allowed by USA Wrestling if prescribed by a doctor or by the chief medical officer of the event. Forbidden in international events.

Fall Victory by pinning an opponent's shoulders to the mat.

FILA *Fédération Internationale des Luttes Associées.* The international governing body of wrestling.

FILA Junior World The 17-20 age group. (Wrestlers 16 years old may enter this division with a medical certificate.)

Fleeing a hold Leaving the wrestling area. Avoiding your opponent's attack. Punished with a caution, a penalty point, and choice of position to your opponent. Two penalty points if fleeing occurs from a danger position.

Freestyle One of the two international wrestling styles. Use of the legs is permitted.

Folkstyle The wrestling style at U.S. schools and colleges. Very active, with holds allowed above and below the waist.

Grand amplitude hold A high, sweeping throw in which you lift your opponent completely off the mat.

Greco-Roman One of the two international styles. Attacking your opponent's legs, or using your own legs in an attack, is prohibited.

Gut wrench A hold using the defensive opponent's torso and turning him to score points.

Handkerchief Each wrestler must have one and must show it to the referee when he gets to the mat.

Headgear Ear protectors. Recommended by USA Wrestling at the Junior and younger levels.

Optional for FILA Juniors and Seniors, if the opponent does not object. Forbidden in international events.

Illegal hold A hold or maneuver forbidden by the rules. Punishment is a caution and one or two penalty points.

Injury time Bout interrupted because a wrestler is injured. Two minutes total allowed each contestant in one bout.

Instantaneous fall The simultaneous touch of both shoulders by either wrestler. Not a fall. Two points for the opponent.

International styles Freestyle and Greco-Roman.

Judge One of the officials, seated across from the mat chairman and timer. The judge assists the referee, awards points, and keeps score.

Junior Nationally, a high school wrestler attending grades 9, 10, 11, or 12 during the school term of the event (or immediately before a summer event), and less than 19 years old on September 1 of the event.

Jury The referee, judge, and mat chairman. The officiating team.

Jury of Appeal The protest committee.

Kids The USA Wrestling division for wrestlers age 14 and younger.

Mandatory rest	A wrestler must have at least 30 minutes after a bout before he can compete again. For high school bouts, the rest must be 45 minutes.
Mat chairman	Chief of the three-man officiating team. He decides on the score or action if the referee and judge disagree.
Medical certificate	Written statement from a physician that a contestant is capable of competing.
Medical examination	A doctor checks each wrestler for skin infections or contagious disease right before the first weigh-in.
Medical officer	A physician, trainer, or other medical professional who treats injuries suffered by the contestants.
Modifications	Variations in the FILA rules adopted by USA Wrestling for domestic competitions and applied to specific age groups.
MSA	Acronym for motion, strength, and alternative exercise as a way to rehabilitate an injury.
NCAA	National Collegiate Athletic Association. The official governing body for college and university wrestling in the United States.
Olympic division	The 19-and-over age group. Wrestlers 17-18 may enter with a medical certificate. Also called Open or Senior division.
On deck	Two wrestlers waiting their turn for the next bout on the same mat.

Outstanding wrestler	The most skilled competitor in an event receives this award.
Overtime	Occurs when the leading wrestler has not scored three technical points, or the score is tied at the end of the regulation bout.
Paddles	Red, white, and blue scoring devices, similar to table tennis paddles, used by the judge and mat chairman to indicate their decisions.
Par terre	When both contestants are wrestling down on the mat, literally "on the ground."
Passivity	Stalling and avoiding combat. Penalized by warnings, and the passive wrestler is placed underneath in the *par terre* position.
Passivity zone	A 1-meter wide band inside the edge of the mat. When the referee shouts "Zone!" the wrestlers must work toward the center of the mat.
Pool	Group.
Protection area	Out-of-bounds area of the mat.
Protest	A formal appeal to reverse a decision, claiming an error.
Referee	The official who runs the bout on the mat. Starts and stops action. Signals his decisions on points, position, and passivity to the judge and the mat chairman.
Reversal	When the wrestler underneath reverses his position and comes to the top position in control. One point value.

RICE   Acronym for rest, ice, compression, and elevation. The suggested formula for immediate management of an injury.

Risk   The concept that a wrestler cannot succeed without taking chances. Refusing to take risks is passivity.

Round   A series of bouts involving all the wrestlers in a weight class or group, once each.

Scoreboard   Unofficial way to show the score of a bout to the spectators.

Seeding   Pre-tournament ranking of contestants by past achievement. Separates them in the draw.

Senior   Another name for the Olympic or Open division, ages 19 and up.

Singlet   The one-piece garment worn by the wrestler. Red singlets are worn by odd numbers, blue by even numbers drawn.

Singlet colors   For each bout, one wrestler wears a red singlet, the other a blue singlet. In high school and college, singlets are in school colors.

Slam   Throwing an opponent down with unnecessary force and not going to the mat with him. May be considered brutality. Illegal throw in Kids competition.

Takedown   Wrestler takes his opponent to the mat from a standing position. Earns one point.

Team leader   The person who leads a delegation on an international tour.

Team scoring The ranking of clubs, states ,or other teams determined by points awarded for the success of their wrestlers.

Technical fall A slang term for victory by technical superiority.

Technical points Points scored by the wrestlers for actions and holds during a bout. Penalty points are technical points.

Technical superiority A victory by a margin of 10 or more points.

Tombé French word for fall. The referee says this word to "count" the time for a fall, about one-half second.

Total wrestling The concept that both wrestlers must give maximum effort at all times. (*See* Risk.)

Universal wrestling Use of a wide variety of techniques and holds.

University USA Wrestling division for wrestlers ages 18-24 and whose class has graduated from high school.

USA Wrestling The national governing body for wrestling in the United States. The delegate to the U.S. Olympic Committee and to FILA.

Weigh-in Before a competition, when a wrestler steps on the scale to certify that his weight is not above the limit for the class in which he is entered.

Weight classes Grouping by size for competitions. Divisions are pounds or kilograms.

World Cup A dual meet competition that is held annually with teams from different continents.

Zone Word used and spoken in a loud voice if the wrestlers enter the passivity zone.

International Terms

USA Wrestling	FILA
Announcer	Speaker
Caution	Warning/Caution
Chief pairing master	Secretariat
Disqualification (cautions)	Disqualification
Disqualification (misconduct)	Brutality
Olympic, Open, or Senior div.	Senior division
Order of wrestling	Start list
Overtime	Extension
Paddles	Bats
Pools	Groups
Protest Committee	Jury of Appeal
Round-robin	Group finals
Scratch weight	No tolerance
Start sheet	Programme
Technical fall	Technical superiority
Warning	Passivity
Weight allowance	Tolerance

12

Olympic and Wrestling Organizations

The organization of, and participation in, the Olympic Games requires the cooperation of a number of independent organizations.

The International Olympic Committee (IOC)

The IOC is responsible for determining where the Games will be held. It is also the obligation of its membership to uphold the principles of the Olympic Ideal and Philosophy beyond any personal, religious, national, or political interest. The IOC is responsible for sustaining the Olympic Movement.

The members of the IOC are individuals who act as the IOC's representatives in their respective countries, not as delegates of their countries within the IOC. The members meet once a year at the IOC Session. They retire at the end of the calendar year in which they turn 70 years old, unless they were elected before the opening of the 110th Session (December 11, 1999). In that case, they must retire at the age of 80. Members elected before 1966 are members for life. The IOC chooses and elects its members from among such persons as its nominations committee considers qualified. There are currently 113 members and 19 honorary members.

The International Olympic Committee's address is—

Chateau de Vidy, CH-1007
Lausanne, Switzerland
Tel: (41-21) 621-6111   Fax: (41-21) 621-6216
www.olympics.org

The National Olympic Committees

Olympic Committees have been created, with the design and objectives of the IOC, to prepare national teams to participate in the Olympic Games. Among the tasks of these committees is to promote the Olympic Movement and its principles at the national level.

The national committees work closely with the IOC in all aspects related to the Games. They are also responsible for applying the rules concerning eligibility of athletes for the Games. Today there are more than 150 national committees throughout the world.

The U.S. Olympic Committee's address is—

Olympic House
One Olympic Plaza
Colorado Springs, CO 80909-5760
Tel: (719) 632-5551   Fax: (719) 578-6216
www.olympic-usa.org

Wrestling Organizations

USA Wrestling
6155 Lehman Drive
Colorado Springs, CO 80918
Tel: (719) 598-8181   Fax: (719) 598-9440
www.usawrestling.com

Fédération Internationale des Luttes Associées
International Federation of Associated Wrestling Styles
Avenue Juste-Olivier 17 CH-1006
Lausanne / Switzerland
Tel: (41.21) 312 84 26   Fax: (41.21) 323 60 73
www.fila-wrestling.org

National Collegiate Athletic Association (NCAA)
700 W. Washington Street
Box 6222
Indianapolis, IN 46206-6222
Tel: (317) 917-6222   Fax: 317/917-6888
www.ncaa.org

National Collegiate Wrestling Association (NCWA)
11411 North Central Suite # 100 W
Dallas, TX. 75243
Tel: (214) 378-8700 ext. 107   Fax: (214) 378-9900
www.ncwa.net

National Wrestling Hall of Fame
405 W. Hall of Fame
Stillwater, OK 74075
Tel: 405-377-5243   Fax: (405)377-5244
www.wrestlinghalloffame.org

US Wrestling Officials Association (USWOA)
2616 Hamilton Ave.
Glenshaw, PA 15116
http://www.usawrestling.org/officials/uswoa_home.htm
Email:uswoaoffice@home.com

13

Olympic Medal Winners

Olympic Wrestling Champions 1968-1996

1968 Mexico City, Mexico
Freestyle champions

114.5 lb	Shigeo Nakata (Japan)
125.5 lb	Yojiro Uetake (Japan)
139 lb	Masaaki Kaneko (Japan)
154.5 lb	Abdollah Movahhed (Iran)
172 lb	Mahmut Ataly (Turkey)
192 lb	Boris Burevich (Soviet Union)
214 lb	Ahmet Ayik (Turkey)
Hwt.	Alexander Medved (Soviet Union)

Greco-Roman champions

114.4 lb	Peter Kirov (Bulgaria)
125.5 lb	Janos Varga (Hungary)
139 lb	Roman Rurua (Soviet Union)
154.5 lb	Munji Mumemura (Japan)
172 lb	Rudolf Vesper (East Germany)
192 lb	Lothar Metz (East Germany)
214 lb	Boyan Radev (Bulgaria)
Hwt.	Istvan Kozma (Hungary)

1972 Munich, Germany

Freestyle champions

105.5 lb	Roman Dmitriev (Soviet Union)
114.5 lb	Kiyomi Kato (Japan)
125.5 lb	Hideaki Yanagida (Japan)
136.5 lb	Zagalav Abdulbekov (Soviet Union)
149.5 lb	Dan Gable (USA)
163 lb	Wayne Wells (USA)
180.5 lb	Levan Tediashvili (Soviet Union)
198 lb	Ben Peterson (USA)
220 lb	Ivan Yarygin (Soviet Union)
Hwt.	Alexander Medved (Soviet Union)

Greco-Roman champions

105.5 lb	Gheorghe Berceanu (Romania)
114.5 lb	Peter Korov (Bulgaria)
125.5 lb	Rustem Kazakov (Soviet Union)
136.5 lb	Georgi Markov (Bulgaria)
149.5 lb	Shamil Khisamutidnov (Soviet Union)
163 lb	Vitezslav Macha (Czechoslovakia)
180.5 lb	Csaba Hegedus (Hungary)
198 lb	Valery Rezantsev (Soviet Union)
220 lb	Nicolae Martinecu (Romania);
Hwt.	Anatoly Roshin (Soviet Union)

1976 Montreal, Canada

Freestyle champions

105.5 lb	Hasan Isaev (Bulgaria)
114.5 lb	Yuji Takada (Japan)
125.5 lb	Vladimir Umin (Soviet Union)
136.5 lb	Yang Jung-Mo (South Korea)
149.5 lb	Pavel Pinigin (Soviet Union)
163 lb	Jiichiro Date (Japan)
180.5 lb	John Peterson (USA)
198 lb	Levan Tediashvili (Soviet Union)
220 lb	Ivan Yarygin (Soviet Union)
Hwt.	Soslan Andiev (Soviet Union)

Greco-Roman champions

105.5 lb	Alexei Shumakov (Soviet Union)
114.5 lb	Vitaly Konstantinov (Soviet Union)
125.5 lb	Pettri Ukkola (Finland)
136.5 lb	Kazimierz Lipien (Poland)
149.5 lb	Suren Nalbandyan (Soviet Union)
163 lb	Anatoly Bykov (Soviet Union)
180.5 lb	Momir Petkovic (Yugoslavia)
198 lb	Valery Rezantsev (Soviet Union)
220 lb	Nikolai Balboshin (Soviet Union)
Hwt.	Alexander Kolchinsky (Soviet Union)

1980 Moscow, Soviet Union

Freestyle champions

105.5 lb	Claudio Pollio (Italy)
114.5 lb	Anatoli Beloglazov (Soviet Union)
125.5 lb	Sergei Beloglazov (Soviet Union)
136.5 lb	Magomedgasan Abushev (Soviet Union)
149.5 lb	Saipulla Absaidov (Soviet Union)
163 lb	Valentin Angelov (Bulgaria)
180.5 lb	Ismail Abilov (Bulgaria)
198 lb	Sanasar Oganesyan (Soviet Union)
220 lb	Ilya Mate (Soviet Union)
Hwt.	Soslan Andiev (Soviet Union)

Greco-Roman champions

105.5 lb	Zaksylik Ushkempirov (Soviet Union)
114.5 lb	Vakhtang Blagidze (Soviet Union)
125.5 lb	Shamil Serikov (Soviet Union)
136.5 lb	Sylianos Mygiakis (Greece)
149.5 lb	Stefan Rusu (Romania)
163 lb	Ferenc Kocsis (Hungary)
180.5 lb	Gennady Korban (Soviet Union)
198 lb	Norbert Novenyi (Hungary)
220 lb	Georgi Raikov (Bulgaria)
Hwt.	Alexander Kolchinsky (Soviet Union)

1984 Los Angeles, USA
Freestyle champions

105.5 lb	Bobby Weaver (USA)
114.5 lb	Saban Trstena (Yugoslavia)
125.5 lb	Hideaki Tomiyama (Japan)
136.5 lb	Randy Lewis (USA)
149.5 lb	You In-Tak (South Korea)
163 lb	Dave Schultz (USA)
180.5 lb	Mark Schultz (USA)
198 lb	Ed Banach (USA)
220 lb	Lou Banach (USA)
Hwt.	Bruce Baumgartner (USA)

Greco-Roman champions

105.5 lb	Vincenzo Maenza (Italy)
114.5 lb	Atsuji Miyahara (Japan)
125.5 lb	Pasquale Passarelli (West Germany)
136.5 lb	Kim Weon-Kee (South Korea)
149.5 lb	Vlado Lisjak (Yugoslavia)
163 lb	Juoko Salomaki (Finland)
180.5 lb	Ion Draica (Romania)
198 lb	Steve Fraser (USA)
220 lb	Vasile Andrei (Romania)
Hwt.	Jeff Blatnick (USA)

1988 Seoul, South Korea
Freestyle champions

105.5 lb	Takashi Kobiashi (Japan)
114.5 lb	Mitsuru Sato (Japan)
125.5 lb	Sergei Beloglazov (Soviet Union)
136.5 lb	John Smith (USA)
149.5 lb	Arsen Fadzaev (Soviet Union)
163 lb	Kenny Monday (USA)
180.5 lb	Han Myung-Woo (South Korea)
198 lb	Makharbek Khadartsev (Soviet Union)
220 lb	Vasile Puscasu (Romania)
286 lb	David Gobedjishvili (Soviet Union)

Greco-Roman champions

105.5 lb	Vincenco Maenza (Italy)
114.5 lb	Jon Ronningen (Norway)
125.5 lb	Andras Sike (Hungary)
136.5 lb	Kamandar Madzidov (Soviet Union)
149.5 lb	Levon Djufalakian (Soviet Union)
163 lb	Kim Young-Nam (South Korea)
180.5 lb	Mikhail Mamiashvili (Soviet Union)
198 lb	Atanas Komchev (Bulgaria)
220 lb	Andrzej Wronski (Poland)
286 lb	Alexander Karelin (Soviet Union)

1992 Barcelona, Spain

Freestyle champions

105.5 lb	Kim Il (North Korea)
114.5 lb	Li Hak-Son (North Korea)
125.5 lb	Alejandro Puerto (Cuba)
136.5 lb	John Smith (USA)
149.5 lb	Arsen Fadzaev (Unified Team)
163 lb	Park Jang-Soon (South Korea)
180.5 lb	Kevin Jackson (USA)
198 lb	Makharbek Khadartsev (Unified Team)
220 lb	Leri Khabelov (Unified Team)
286 lb	Bruce Baumgartner (USA)

Greco-Roman champions

105.5 lb	Oleg Koucherenko (Unified Team)
114.5 lb	Jon Ronningen (Norway)
125.5 lb	An Han-Bong (South Korea)
136.5 lb	Mehmet Akif Pirim (Turkey)
149.5 lb	Atilla Repka (Hungary)
163 lb	Mnatsakan Iskandarian (Unified Team)
180.5 lb	Peter Farkus (Hungary)
198 lb	Maik Bullman (Germany)
220 lb	Hector Millian (Cuba)
286 lb	Alexander Karelin (Unified Team)

1996 Atlanta, USA
Freestyle champions

105.5 lb	Kim Il (North Korea)
114.5 lb	V. Dimitrov Jordanov (Bulgaria)
125.5 lb	Kendall Cross (USA)
136.5 lb	Tom Brands (USA)
149.5 lb	Vadim Bogiev (Unified Team)
163 lb	Buvaysa Saytyev (Unified Team)
180.5 lb	Khadzhimurad Magomedov (Unified Team)
198 lb	Rasull Khadem (Iran)
220 lb	Kurt Angle (USA)
286 lb	Mahmut Demir (Turkey)

Greco-Roman champions

105.5 lb	Sim Kwon Ho (Korea)
114.5 lb	Armen Nazarian (Armenia)
125.5 lb	Yuriy Melnitchenko (Kazakhstan)
136.5 lb	Wlodzimierz Zawadzki (Poland)
149.5 lb	Ryszard Wolny (Poland)
163 lb	Filiberto Azcuy (Cuba)
180.5 lb	Hamza Yerlikaya (Turkey)
198 lb	Vyacheslav Oleynyk (Ukraine)
220 lb	Andrzej Wronski (Poland)
286 lb	Alexander Karelin (Unified Team)

Wrestling Medal Winners by Country, 1896-2000

Year	Freestyle	Greco-Roman	Overall
1896	No event	Germany	No award
1904	USA	no event	No award
1906	No event	Austria	No award
1908	Gr. Britain	Finland	Gr. Britain
1912	No event	Finland	No award
1920	USA and Finland	Finland	Finland
1924	USA	Finland	Finland
1928	Finland	Germany	Finland
1932	USA	Sweden	Sweden
1936	USA	Sweden	Sweden
1948	Turkey	Sweden	Turkey
1952	Sweden	USSR	USSR
1956	Iran	USSR	USSR
1960	Turkey	USSR	Turkey
1964	Bulgaria	USSR	USSR
1968	Japan	USSR	USSR
1972	USSR	USSR	USSR
1976	USSR	USSR	USSR
1980	USSR	USSR	USSR
1984	USA	Romania	USA
1988	USSR	USSR	USSR
1992	Unified Team	Unified Team	Unified Team
1996	USA	Poland	USA
2000	Russia	Russia	Russia

No Olympic Games were held in 1916 during World War I or in 1940 and 1944 during World War II.

14

2000 Olympic Games

The Summer Olympic Games in Sydney featured sixteen medal events in wrestling, divided evenly between Greco-Roman and freestyle. Russian wrestlers dominated the competition, winning nine medals, six of them gold. The United States came in second with seven medals, and Cuba finished third with five. A highlight for the U.S. team was the victory by Rulon Gardner over the extraordinary Russian champion Alexander Karelin—one of the great upsets in recent Olympic history.

Greco-Roman

54 kg (119 lb)

Sim Kwon Ho of South Korea won his second gold medal in Greco-Roman wrestling by defeating world champion Lazaro Rivas of Cuba, 8-0. Kwon Ho's first gold came at the 1996 Games, and he nearly won his 2000 crown by grand superiority. The bronze went to Kang Yong Gyun of North Korea, who defeated the Ukraine's Andriy Kalashnikov, 7-0.

58 kg (128 lb)

Bulgaria's Armen Nazarian won the gold over Kim In-Sub of South Korea by a fall. The bronze medal went to Sheng Zetian of China, who defeated Rifat Yildiz of Germany, 2-0, in overtime.

63 kg (139 lb)

A 22-year-old Russian, Varteres Samourgachev, the European champion, defeated Juan Luis Maren of Cuba by 3-0 in the gold medal match, which went to overtime. This year marked Samourgachev's Olympic debut, but he showed no signs of nervousness. The bronze went to Akaki Chachua of Georgia, who defeated Beat Motzer of Switzerland by a fall.

69 kg (152 lb)

Filiberto Azcuy of Cuba won with greater superiority (11-0) to beat Japan's Katsuhiko Nagata for the gold medal. The bronze went to Alexei Glouchkov of Russia, who won out over Valeri Nikitin of Estonia, 5-0.

76 kg (167 lb)

Mourat Kardanov of Russia, known for his fierce "gut wrencher" holds, defeated American Matt Lindland by 3-0 for the gold. Marko Yli-Hannuksela of Finland won the bronze, defeating David Manukyan of Ukraine by a score of 4-2.

85 kg (187 lb)

Turkey's Hamza Yerlikaya won the gold in this weight category over Sandor Istvan Bardosi of Hungary. Mukhran Vakhtangadze of Georgia won the bronze over Fritz Aanes of Norway, 4-0.

97 kg (213 lb)

Former world champion Mikael Ljungberg of Sweden won the gold by 2-1 in overtime, defeating Davyd Saldadze of Ukraine. The bronze went to an American, Garrett Lowney, who defeated Konstantinos Thanos of Greece by 3-1 in another overtime match.

130 kg (286 lb)

In a remarkable upset, American Rulon Gardner defeated Russia's Alexander Karelin, who is considered the greatest Olympic wrestler of modern times and had not lost a single bout since 1987. Karelin, the nine-time world champion, was looking for his fourth consecutive Olympic gold medal in the 130 kg, or super heavyweight, division. Gardner's strategy was to wear down his opponent, yet not allow himself to relax or get thrown. He accomplished what he set out to do, although neither wrestler had the 3 points needed at the end of regulation. With five seconds left in the overtime period, Karelin surrendered. The bronze medal was won by Dmitry Debelka of Belarus, who beat Israel's Juri Yevseychyc in overtime, 1-0.

Freestyle

54 kg (119 lb)

Namig Abdullayev of Azerbaijan won the gold by defeating Sammie Henson of the United States in a closely contested 4-3 match. The bronze went to Amiran Karntanov of Greece, who defeated German Kontoev of Belarus, 5-4.

58 kg (128 lb)

The gold medal went to Alireza Dabir of Iran, who defeated the Ukrainian Yevgen Buslovych, 3-0. The bronze was won by American Terry Brands, who defeated Damir Zakhartdinov of Uzbekistan, 3-2.

63 kg (139 lb)

Russia's Mourad Oumakhanov won the gold medal over Bulgaria's Serafim Barzakov, 3-2. Jang Jae Sung of South Korea captured the bronze by defeating Mohammad Talaei of Iran, 12-2, with greater superiority.

69 kg (152 lb)

Canada's Daniel Igali defeated Russia's Arsen Gitinov, 7-4, to win the gold medal. The bronze went to Lincoln McIlravy of the United States, who beat Sergei Demchenko of Belarus, 3-1.

76 kg (167 lb)

Alexander Leipold of Germany defeated American Brandon Slay, 4-0, for the gold medal. The bronze medal went to Moon Eui Jae of South Korea, who defeated Adem Bereket of Turkey by a fall.

85 kg (187 lb)

Adam Saitiev of Russia defeated Cuba's Yoel Romero by a fall to win the gold. Macedonia's Mogamed Ibragimov won the bronze by besting Iran's Amirreza Khadem Azghadi, 4-1, in overtime.

97 kg (213 lb)

Another Russian, Saghid Mourtasaliyev, defeated Kazakhstan's Islam Bairamukov, 6-0, for the gold. The bronze went to Eldar Kurtanidze of Georgia, who bested Poland's Marek Garmulewicz, 4-1.

130 kg (286 lb)

Russia's David Moussoulbes defeated Uzbekistan's Artur Taymazov by a score of 5-2 to win the gold medal. The bronze went to Cuba's Alexis Rodriguez, who defeated Abbas Jadidi of Iran in overtime, 1-0.